Health Information Technology Evaluation Handbook

From Meaningful Use to Meaningful Outcome

Health Information Technology Evaluation Handbook

From Meaningful Use to
Meaningful Outcome

By
Vitaly Herasevich and Brian W. Pickering

CRC Press is an imprint of the
Taylor & Francis Group, an **informa** business
A PRODUCTIVITY PRESS BOOK

CRC Press
Taylor & Francis Group
6000 Broken Sound Parkway NW, Suite 300
Boca Raton, FL 33487-2742

© 2018 by Taylor & Francis Group, LLC

CRC Press is an imprint of Taylor & Francis Group, an Informa business

No claim to original U.S. Government works

Printed on acid-free paper

International Standard Book Number-13: 978-1-4987-6647-0 (Hardback)
International Standard Book Number-13: 978-1-315-15385-8 (eBook)

Visit the Taylor & Francis Web site at
http://www.taylorandfrancis.com

and the CRC Press Web site at
http://www.crcpress.com

Contents

Foreword xi

Preface xiii

Authors xxiii

1   The Foundation and Pragmatics of HIT Evaluation ... 1
   1.1   Need for Evaluation 1
          Historical Essay 3
   1.2   HIT: Why Should We Worry about It? 4
          Historical Essay 7
          Definitions 7
          History of Technology Assessment 9
          Medical or Health Technology Assessment 9
          Health Information Technology Assessment 10
   1.3   Regulatory Framework in the United States 11
          Food and Drug Administration 12
          Agency for Healthcare Research and Quality 13
   1.4   Fundamental Steps Required for Meaningful
          HIT Evaluation 14
          Suggested Reading 17
          References 17

2   Structure and Design of Evaluation Studies 19
   2.1   Review of Study Methodologies and Approaches
          That Can Be Used in Health IT Evaluations 19
          Define the Health IT (Application, System) to
             Be Studied 20

Define the Stakeholders Whose Questions
  Should Be Addressed 20
Define and Prioritize Study Questions....................21
2.2 Clinical Research Design Overview.........................23
Clinical Epidemiology Evidence Pyramid...............24
Specific Study Design Considerations in Health
  IT Evaluation...27
Randomized Controlled Trial in Health IT 29
Diagnostic Performance Study 31
2.3 How to Ask Good Evaluation Questions and
  Develop Protocol...31
Suggested Reading...35
References..36

3 Study Design and Measurements Fundamentals ...37
3.1 Fundamental Principles of Study Design 39
Selection Criteria and Sample...............................39
Validity 41
Accuracy and Precision...42
Bias 44
Confounding..45
Measurement Variables 45
3.2 Core Measurements in HIT Evaluation....................47
Clinical Outcome Measures 48
Clinical Process Measurements.............................. 48
Financial Impact Measures 49
Other Outcome Measurement Concepts 51
    Intermediate Outcome 51
    Composite Outcome...51
    Patient-Reported Outcomes 51
    Health-Related Quality of Life........................52
    Subjective and Objective Measurements.......52
3.3 Data Collection for Evaluation Studies 53
3.4 Data Quality 54
Suggested Reading...56
References..56

4   Analyzing the Results of Evaluation 59
　4.1　Fundamental Principles of Statistics 60
　　　Data Preparation 61
　　　Descriptive (Summary) Statistics 61
　　　Data Distribution 61
　　　Confidence Intervals 64
　　　p-Value 65
　4.2　Statistical Tests: Choosing the Right Test 66
　　　Hypothesis Testing 66
　　　Non-Parametric Tests 67
　　　One- and Two-Tailed Tests 67
　　　Paired and Independent Tests 68
　　　Number of Comparisons Groups 68
　　　Analytics Methods 70
　　　　　Identifying Relationship: Correlation 70
　　　　　Regression 70
　　　　　Longitudinal Studies: Repeated Measures 71
　　　　　Time-to-Event: Survival Analysis 72
　　　　　Diagnostic Accuracy Studies 72
　　　　　Assessing Agreements 74
　　　　　Outcome Measurements 74
　　　　　Other Statistical Considerations 77
　　　　　Multiple Comparisons 77
　　　　　Subgroup Analysis 77
　　　　　Sample Size Calculation 78
　　　　　Commonly Used Statistical Tools 78
　　　Suggested Reading 79
　　　References 80

**5   Proposing and Communicating the Results of
      Evaluation Studies 83**
　5.1　Target Audience 84
　5.2　Methods of Dissemination 84
　5.3　Universal, Scientifically Based Outline for the
　　　Dissemination of Evaluation Study Results 86
　5.4　Reporting Standards and Guidelines 91

5.5 Other Communication Methods 96
Suggested Reading 102
Books on the Presentation Design 103
References.. 104

6 Safety Evaluation 105
6.1 Role of Government Organizations in HIT
Safety Evaluation 106
ONC EHR Technology Certification Program........ 109
Meaningful Use (Stage 2) and 2014 Edition
Standards and Certification Criteria 109
Safety Evaluation outside the Legislative
Process... 109
6.2 Problem Identification and Related Metrics:
What Should One Study?.. 111
Where Can One Study the Safety Evaluation of
HIT? Passive and Active Evaluation 113
6.3 Tools and Methodologies to Assist Capture and
Report HIT Safety Events: Passive Evaluation 116
Simulation Studies and Testing in a Safe
Environment: Active Evaluations 120
6.4 Summary.. 122
Suggested Reading 123
References.. 123

7 Cost Evaluation 125
7.1 Health Economics Basics 127
Setting and Methodology.. 129
What to Measure and Outcomes............................ 131
7.2 Main Types of Cost Analysis Applied to HIT......... 133
Cost-Benefit Analysis 133
Cost-Effectiveness Analysis.................................... 134
Cost-Minimization Analysis.................................... 136
Return on Investment 137
How to Report Economic Evaluation Studies........ 138
Suggested Reading.. 144
References.. 144

8 Efficacy and Effectiveness Evaluation.................. 147
   8.1   Clinically Oriented Outcomes of Interest (What)... 150
   8.2   Settings for Evaluation (Where) 152
   8.3   Evaluation Methods (How)..................................... 153
   8.4   Evaluation Timing (When)...................................... 155
   8.5   Example of HIT Evaluation Studies....................... 155
           Example of a Survey Analysis Study...................... 155
           Example of a Gold Standard Validation Study 157
           Example of a Before-After Study............................ 158
   8.6   Security Evaluation... 159
           Suggested Reading 161
           References.. 162

9 Usability Evaluation 163
   9.1   Evaluation of Efficiency... 164
   9.2   Effectiveness and Evaluation of Errors 165
   9.3   Evaluating Consistency of Experience (User
           Satisfaction)...166
   9.4   Electronic Medical Record Usability Principles 168
   9.5   Usability and the EHR Evaluation Process 170
           A Note on Evaluating the Real-World Usability
               of HIT... 171
   9.6   Usability Testing Approaches................................. 173
   9.7   Specific Usability Testing Methods 175
           Cognitive Walk-Through... 175
               Key Features and Output.............................. 176
   9.8   Procedure.. 176
           Phase 1: Defining the Users of the System............ 176
           Phase 2: Defining the Task(s) for the Walk-
               Through 176
           Phase 3: Walking through the Actions and
               Critiquing Critical Information 177
           Phase 4: Summarization of the Walk-Through
               Results 177
           Phase 5: Recommendations to Designers.............. 177
           Keystroke-Level Model... 178

Key Features and Output 178
Heuristic Evaluation 179
Key Features and Output 179
Reporting 181
System Usability Scale 181
Benefits of Using an SUS 181
9.9 Conclusions 183
Suggested Reading 184
References 184
10 Case Studies 187
10.1 Case Study 1: SWIFT Score 188
Rationale 188
SWIFT Score Development 188
SWIFT Implementation 189
Results 190
Case Discussion 190
SWIFT Score 191
Study Design 191
Implementation 192
Results 193
10.2 Case Study 2: Lessons Applied, More to Be
Learned—AWARE Dashboard 194
AWARE Design Principals 195
Testing 197
AWARE Implementation 197
Results and Lessons Learned 199
10.3 Summary 201
References 201
Index 203

Foreword

The United States has undergone a sea change with respect to electronic health record (EHR) adoption. While just a few years ago, the proportion of hospitals and physician offices using EHRs was less than a third, it is now over 90% in both sectors. In the inpatient setting, with about a half-dozen vendors having the vast majority of the market share, the figure is over 200 in this setting. Yet, while most providers are using EHRs, they are often not getting the value they have wanted to receive.

So why is that? The main reason is that much of this software is highly configurable, and organizations can get either quite good or very poor results depending on how they set up their configuration. To know how you are doing, it is absolutely essential to be able to monitor what your results are, and it is also important to be able to make some changes yourself to improve performance. Thus, this book by Herasevich and Pickering fills an important niche, and one that will be important for all organizations, not just the select few.

Traditionally, health technology evaluation has often been device oriented, with a high degree of regulation. But software is hard to regulate, and the Food and Drug Administration has taken a light hand. Implementations—and thus the impact—of clinical information technology vary a great deal from site to site.

It has also been a challenge to get the information one needs to know to perform evaluations in one place, and this book is an attempt to provide that. Herasevich and Pickering have long been innovators in using health information technology (HIT) to improve care in a variety of settings, especially the intensive care unit. They have learned through the school of hard knocks about how to evaluate HIT, and the importance of doing so. We have often found in our own evaluations that things did not turn out the way we expected—some things we thought would be "slam dunks" failed miserably, and decision support that was working well suddenly stopped having the desired impact. In this book, Herasevich and Pickering describe the key concepts around scientifically evaluating the impact of HIT applications of a variety of types. Every institution will need to have people with this skill set if they want to get the improvements in safety, quality, and value that they are hoping for with their HIT implementations and this book will be a very helpful tool for them.

David W. Bates, MD, MSc
Chief, Division of General Internal Medicine,
Brigham and Women's Hospital

Medical Director of Clinical and Quality
Analysis, Partners Healthcare

Professor of Medicine, Harvard Medical School

Professor, Department of Health Policy and Management,
Harvard School of Public Health

Preface

Motivation and Background

> The best interest of the patient is the only interest to be considered.
>
> **William J. Mayo**
> *1910*

At its best, medicine is all about the patient. Since the time of Hippocrates, the human connection between patient and healthcare provider has been central to the provision of high-quality care. Recently, a third party—the electronic health record—has been inserted into the middle of that relationship. Governments and clinical providers are investing billions of dollars in health information technologies (HIT) in the expectation that this will translate into healthier patients experiencing better care at lower cost. The scale of adoption, driven by a combination of marketplace incentives and penalties, is breathtaking.

In the initial push to roll out HIT, the view that patients would benefit and costs be contained was widely advanced. The argument for adoption usually went something like this: See the handwritten prescription for patient medications, and note the illegibility of the drug name, drug dose, and lack of frequency or route of administration information. Next, see the electronic form, a legible, precise, complete electronic prescription. Case closed. The face validity of the argument was compelling—doctors' terrible handwriting causes medication errors and can be eliminated with electronic prescribing. The logic driving this argument, when widely applied, presented a story that made sense to many. How could a digital revolution in medicine not help?

A tipping point was reached with the introduction of the Health Information Technology for Economic and Clinical Health (HITECH) Act in 2009. This landmark piece of legislation was presented to the world as the foundation of healthcare reform. Since then, an estimated $35 billion has been diverted to investment in health information technology. As we write this book, widespread adoption of health information systems is a reality, and we are coming to the end of the first wave of implementation and use. The digital revolution is here, and the claims made on behalf of the unexpected guest sitting in on the consultation between the patient and the clinician deserves systematic scrutiny! It is time to take stock of what we have gained, what we have lost, and what we should expect in the future.

As the initial HITECH investment dries up, we are entering a phase of market saturation for HIT commercial systems. Competition in this space will lead to innovation and a proliferation of new technologies with difficult-to-predict effects on providers, patients, and health systems. Even as we dissect the meaningful use provisions of the HITECH Act for lessons learned, the question of how HIT affects patients, quality of healthcare, and clinical providers has been poorly answered. Surprisingly little has been published on the topic of the clinical effects of HIT.

When we let it, technology in healthcare can produce rapid advancements, but HIT is far from a plug-and-play technology. As such, the complexity of implementation can quickly overwhelm an organization, consuming a disproportionate amount of attention. In the scramble to meet the requirements and time line stipulated by a HIT commercial partner, the focus can drift away from the needs of the patient and clinical practice. To paraphrase Hippocrates, "It is far more important to know the context in which health information technology will be used than to know the specifics of the technology." Understanding that context and the problems to be solved requires tapping into the wisdom of our frontline providers and patients.

A systematic approach to the evaluation of technology in healthcare is needed if we are to reliably discriminate between useful innovation and clever marketing. This book is an attempt to provide guidance to any individual or organization wishing to take control of the conversation and to objectively evaluate a technology on their own terms.

We wrote this book with an emphasis on a clinically oriented, data-driven approach to the evaluation of HIT solutions. This will allow the reader to set the evaluation agenda and help avoid situations in which the needs of the patient or clinical practice play a secondary role to the needs identified by technical experts and engineers.

Need for the Book: What Will the Reader Learn?

The structured evaluation of a project's effects is an essential element of the justification for investment in HIT. A systematic approach to evaluation and testing should allow for comparison between different HIT interventions with the goal of identifying and promoting those that improve clinical care or other outcomes of interest. The question of the day is no longer "why" but "how" can healthcare professionals, organizations, and patients evaluate their health information technologies. Evaluating and predicting a project's impact is best done with input from as broad a range of stakeholders as possible. Therefore, it is in everyone's interest to have a working knowledge of HIT evaluation methods. The stakes are too high for the consumer to take at face value the claims made about technology in the healthcare sector. This book provides an easy-to-read reference outlining the basic concepts, theory, and methods required to perform a systematic evaluation of HIT for a given clinical purpose.

We cover key domains in HIT evaluation: study structure and design, measurement fundamentals, results analysis, communicating results, guideline development, and reference standards. Thus, in the chapters that follow, we outline step-by-step, core knowledge and tools that we or others have used successfully to evaluate the impact of technology on real-world healthcare problems. We explain how statistics is important in HIT evaluation and how to interpret key reported metrics. We introduce study design, examples of useful measurement tools, and an outline of how to report your findings to your intended audience. At the end of the book, we tie the evaluation methodologies together with a couple of real-life examples from research and practice. We do not attempt to provide an exhaustive guide to each of the topics touched on in the chapters, but we do provide references to some excellent courses and books on specific topics for those who wish to dig deeper.

Why Is This Book Unique?

Of course, HIT evaluation means different things to different stakeholders. When we look at the existing literature on this broad topic, many scientific publications focus on evaluation needs from the perspective of regulatory bodies. Our own summaries of knowledge for our own use in the field of applied clinical informatics resulted in this book.

We are in a very privileged position in our day jobs in an organization with a long history of patient-centered care advocacy and innovation in healthcare. Unprecedented growth of the importance of HIT, access to our clinical information systems, and work in an environment that does not obstruct maverick clinicians' direct access to seriously smart IT developers and programmers enable us to bring to life informatics ideas. With a small team of clinicians and IT experts, we were allowed to develop and evaluate a range of HIT solutions into our clinical practice; in the process, we solved some problems identified as important.

This access to IT and clinical resources has greatly informed and helped mature our thoughts and the approach to HIT evaluation outlined in this book. This resulted in a book served up in "tranches," or portions, without any inflation of the manuscript.

How to Use This Book

First, this book is not designed to educate the reader to the level of HIT evaluation ninja after reading it cover to cover. The book outlines the knowledge needed to become an expert in the field and thus acts as a navigational aid. While each chapter is self-contained, we recommend first skimming each chapter for new concepts and referring back to them while reading the examples at the end of the book. The Suggested Reading section at the end of each chapter is suitable for those looking to delve more deeply into particular areas of interest. Ideally, readers will apply the tools and knowledge to projects and research of their own, and arrive at an enriched understanding of their increasingly high tech surroundings. In the process, we hope readers will actively participate in the design and evaluation of their information systems and remain potent advocates for their patients and frontline colleagues.

At the very end of the book, we outline two examples of technologies we deployed into our environments and evaluated. While the first occurred at the beginning of our collaborative research career and the last derives from our most recent collaboration, both demonstrate the fundamental importance of systematic evaluation in a real-world environment with frontline provider feedback. What is true in the design and laboratory phases rarely translates cleanly into the real world. Claims made without objective data gathered from working environments should be treated with skepticism. Failing an objective clinical trial, frontline providers and patients have an excellent instinct for inflated claims, and their feedback should be taken seriously. In this field in particular, it is our overwhelming experience that HIT experts and middle managers are poorly equipped to make reliable judgments regarding the potential utility of a particular technology. Their recommendations, while important, should be taken with a grain of salt if they deviate in any substantial manner from that of the frontline provider or patient. Finally, the goal of the book is to establish a practical agenda for HIT evaluation.

Classroom Potential

This book is in part inspired by a class the authors run each year as part of a Master's in Clinical Research program at Mayo Clinic and by their development of a new curriculum for one of the first clinical informatics fellowship programs they directed at their institution. Readers can use the book itself to develop their own postgraduate HIT evaluation classes.

The Journey of Writing the Book

> It is far more important to know what person the disease has than what disease the person has
>
> **Hippocrates**
> *c. 460–c. 370 BC*

We are believers in the wisdom of crowds! In our experience, the very best questions and solutions derive from the front line of healthcare delivery. HIT investment is a high-stakes game, and health organization leaders are acutely aware that an incorrect decision can come at an enormous cost. Both patients and providers need to be considered the key stake-holders when it comes to the impact of HIT on meaningful outcomes. However, it can be difficult for organizations to incorporate feedback from this group into their decision mak-ing regarding HIT, particularly when that input runs contrary to expert opinion and advice. Therefore, we wanted to deliver a pragmatic guide to HIT evaluation straight into the hands of as many of those key stakeholders as possible.

Our hope is that the collective impact of this book will be greater than that of a comprehensive tome read by a few experts. In demystifying the science of HIT evaluation, we hope to democratize the decision-making process and empower frontline users to ask significant questions of their technology and to articulate their requirements and concerns in a productive manner.

Acknowledgments

We are deeply indebted to our patients and our clinical, infor-mation technology, and academic colleagues. While we have built technology on the shoulders of all who came before us, we would especially like to acknowledge Tiong Ing and Troy Neumann, who were instrumental in transforming our thoughts into concrete and beautiful architecture—without them, this book would not have been possible. To all our clinical colleagues in critical care who have been patient with our experiments and have provided inspiration, support, and startlingly good feedback, we would like to extend a special thank you.

Individuals who went beyond the call and who represent the very best that a patient-centered organization such as ours can offer include

- Dr. Dan Brown, who provided the support needed at the committee level when we became mired in red tape
- Dr. Brad Narr, who not only listened patiently but provided unlimited support, advice, and guidance
- Dr. Steve Peters, the source of all knowledge of health IT goings on in our institution and without whose guidance we would have wandered off the path and into the jungle, never to be seen again
- Dr. Mike Joyner, who connects the dots in a way few humans can
- Dr. Man Li, without whom we would not have an operational HIT research database
- Dr. Rahul Kashyap, who keeps our research infrastructure and fellows on their toes
- Dr. Yue Dong, our friend and colleague, responsible for introducing us to all manner of social media and the concept of simulation for preclinical evaluation of technology
- Dr. Pablo Moreno Franco, a trailblazer and friend
- Super users and extraordinary early adopters of our technologies Theo Loftsgard, Katherine Heise, and many many others

We would like to especially thank our mentor and friend Dr. Ogie Gajic. Ogie has influenced both our careers and lives in indescribable ways. He was not available to help write this book, but all the core concepts outlined here are as attributable to him as they are to us. Research and development in an academic institution can be a bruising and thankless endeavor. We are fortunate to have Ogie as a focus point, to lift us up when we are feeling down, and to shoot us down when we become carried away with ourselves. Ogie, long may our Minnesota journey continue. We are looking forward to seeing the northern lights with you in your beautiful cabin.

Finally, we would very much like to acknowledge our families.

Vitaly Herasevich: Thanks to my ex-wife Dr. Olga Rudnik for the journey during the first part of my life; for two wonderful children, Lev and Sasha; and for kicking me out to spin off the second part of my life journey. Thanks to Dr. Svetlana Boulgakova for recent inspiration I hope will last forever.

Brian Pickering: Where would I be without my wife Dr. Amelia Barwise and our four children, Hannah, Molly, Samuel, and Grace. Amelia has encouraged and supported me through the years, continues to surprise me, and remains my closest friend, greatest ally, and most reliable critic. My thoughts on crowd wisdom are reinforced by my daily experience with our four children and their friends.

Finally, we thank our editor, Kris Mednansky, for her guidance and her patience with accommodating our busy schedules.

Authors

Vitaly Herasevich is an associate professor of anesthesiology and medicine in the Department of Anesthesiology and Perioperative Medicine, Division of Critical Care, Mayo Clinic, Rochester, Minnesota. He has been involved in medical informatics for over 20 years, with a specific concentration on applied clinical informatics in critical care and the science of healthcare delivery.

He was born in Belarus, where he earned his MD and PhD degrees, and joined the Mayo Clinic in 2006. He codirects the Clinical Informatics in Intensive Care program as part of a research group that works to decrease complications and improve outcomes for critically ill patients through systematic research and quality improvement. He is interested in studying and developing clinical syndromic surveillance alerting systems ("sniffers"), clinical data visualization (novel patient-centered electronic medical records), and complex large data warehousing for healthcare predictive and prescriptive analytics as well as outcome reporting. He is co-inventor of a number of technologies including AWARE platform, resulting in technologies commercialization. He has coauthored 80 articles and authored two editions of his book *Computer for Physician*. As part of an education effort, Dr. Herasevich teaches medical informatics classes at the Mayo Medical School and Mayo Graduate School. He is active within informatics and professional societies, serving on a number of committees.

Brian Pickering is an associate professor of anesthesiology in the Department of Anesthesiology and Perioperative Medicine, Division of Critical Care, Mayo Clinic, Rochester, Minnesota. Dr. Pickering was born in Dublin, Ireland. He completed his medical education at Trinity College Dublin prior to his residency and fellowship training in anesthesiology and critical care at the College of Anesthetists, Royal College of Surgeons Ireland. He moved with his family to Rochester, Minnesota, in 2008 to complete further fellowship training in critical care at Mayo Clinic, where he currently practices. Dr. Pickering's primary research area is focused on improving the processes of care in the acute care setting to improve patient health and outcomes while reducing medical costs. Leveraging the sophisticated electronic infrastructure available at Mayo Clinic, Dr. Pickering's laboratory group have developed novel user interfaces, smart alerts, and reporting dashboards that target deviations from best practice and support healthcare providers to deliver a consistently high level of clinical performance to the bedside. With an established culture of innovation and patient-centered care models, the laboratory has unparalleled access to clinicians, clinical settings, homegrown technologies, and clinical information systems. This environment facilitates rapid bedside-to-bench and bench-to-bedside development cycles. The laboratories work has already led to practice improvement in Mayo Clinic ICUs through the implementation and adoption of a number of acute care clinical and administrative applications; several high profile funding awards; and intellectual property, which has been patented and licensed successfully by Mayo Clinic ventures. Together with institutional IT, the multidisciplinary team have developed a platform, AWARE, which addresses key safety concerns including, information overload, errors of omission, and workload associated with electronic medical record use.

Chapter 1

The Foundation
and Pragmatics of
HIT Evaluation

1.1 Need for Evaluation

The introduction of new, disruptive technologies and innovations may bring significant benefits for patients including
enhanced quality of life and more efficient care. Innovations
in clinical practice give healthcare providers the opportunity to
improve the effectiveness and quality of the care they provide
and to apply safer treatment while at the same time improving their job satisfaction. On a national level—and in line with
government objectives—technological innovation may improve
quality of care with better outcomes at reduced costs.

A recent analysis of Healthgrades' hospital performance
database on mortality and complication rates shows that
electronic medical records (EMRs) do have a positive impact
on care.[1] These large-scale, national-level analyses, however,
are prone to use less scientifically sound methodologies and
are not able to answer many other specific questions that

are important for other stakeholders and users of healthcare information technology (HIT or health IT). What is usability in this particular module? What impact on time does that application have? What are the consequences of data misinterpretation? How does system downtime impact clinical procedures?

In 2015, a systematic review and meta-analysis was published dealing with the impact of the EMR on mortality, length of stay, and cost in the hospital and intensive care unit (one of the most data dense clinical environments). This analysis shows that electronic interventions did not have a substantial effect on the metrics reviewed. One of the reasons was the small number of studies that could be systematically aggregated due to the heterogeneity of study populations, interventions, and endpoints.[2]

Current evaluation mostly targets the national level but grossly omits data at the provider and patient level. Many technological innovations seem to offer potential benefits to patients, clinicians, and healthcare in general, but their diffusion can be delayed or omitted due to the absence of evidence regarding specific benefits. A significant number of technologies, however, have not turned out to be important advances. Also, some innovative technologies have the potential to do more harm than have a positive impact.

The field of health technology assessment (HTA) originated in the 1970s, when a growing array of costly medical equipment concerned taxpayers and health insurers regarding their ability and willingness to fund their use.[3]

Ultimately, HTA sought decision-making evidence. In 1970, HTA started synthesizing the available evidence—efficacy and cost-effectiveness of technological interventions—compiling it in a format that was helpful for health policy-makers, mostly at a national level. The field became more mature over the years and spread from the United States to Europe. HTA became more popular in Europe in the 1980s, and increasing effort was devoted to more effectively disseminate information to influence clinicians and local administrators.

Historical Essay

The tobacco smoke enema was a medical procedure that was widely used by Western medical practitioners at the end of the eighteenth century as a treatment for drowsiness, respiratory failure, headaches, stomach cramps, colds, and others conditions.

In 1774, two London-based physicians, William Hawes and Thomas Cogan, formed The Institution for Affording Immediate Relief to Persons Apparently Dead From Drowning. Their practice quickly spread, reaching its peak in the early nineteenth century.

The tobacco smoke enema procedure declined after 1811, when English scientist Ben Brodie discovered nicotine's toxicity to the cardiac system using an animal model.[4]

As technologies and science progress, a tremendous amount of information technology (IT) is being added every year to the HIT space. Recent government incentives combined with technological progress have given additional reasons for clinicians to implement and adopt HIT.

Like medical technologies in the 1970s, however, we have little evidence regarding the specific risks and benefits of HIT. We are in a situation much like the beginning of the nineteenth century, when a single statement, "our software can save lives," is believed and trusted. New medications cannot be introduced to the market without rigorous clinical evaluation (even outside regulatory bodies). While commercial IT products undergo technical validation and testing before being delivered to customers, unfortunately, this testing has nothing to do with clinically oriented metrics such as mortality, complications, medical errors, length of hospitalization, and so on.

Direct users of HIT have the following specific questions that are not answered by technical or policy-oriented evaluation:

1. Is the HIT (software) safe to use on my patients?
2. Does the HIT do what it claims and is designed to do?
3. Is the end result of this technology useful for patients and users?
4. Can this HIT be usefully applied in my specific practice, and what is the cost-benefit of usage?

1.2 HIT: Why Should We Worry about It?

Technological advances combined with government incentives and requirements are providing solid reasons for individual physicians and hospitals to move toward implementing HIT.

The value of the quick-moving information that is provided for decision making, however, is not often supported by evidence. An informed decision regarding the use of new technology is based on solid scientific evidence, not elevated speech. The regulations and requirements for the rapid deployment of software products, however, have a net limiting effect on the ability to evaluate the practical utility of HIT.

Most of the time, when people talk about HIT, they are talking about EMRs. An EMR is defined by the National Alliance for Health Information Technology (NAHIT) as "an electronic record of health-related information on an individual that can be created, gathered, managed, and consulted by authorized clinicians and staff within one health care organization." In contrast, an electronic health record (EHR) is defined as "an electronic record of health-related information on an individual that conforms to nationally recognized interoperability standards and that can be created, managed, and consulted by authorized clinicians and staff across more than one health care organization."

Very often, the terms EMR and EHR are used interchangeably. The principal difference is the interoperability of an EHR.

The ultimate goal of HIT adoption is a health information exchange (HIE), a national infrastructure to provide a network where health information can be exchanged among hospital and physician offices using EMRs. This structure does not exist and is still under development.

The resources for successful EMR deployment and utilization do exist, but many questions arise when considering the end users of such technology.

Do EMRs deliver on their promises? What are the intended and unintended consequences of EMR adoption for healthcare providers?

In a 2015 article published in the *Journal of Medical Economics*, healthcare providers shared opinions about whether EMRs have delivered on promises such as increased efficiency, better time management, and faster charting. The vast majority of clinicians expressed disappointment with EMRs.[5]

Physicians are key stakeholders in the adoption of EMR technologies. Their satisfaction and support of their hospitals' EMR efforts are critical to ensuring EMRs become a positive influence on the hospital environment. Figure 1.1 presents common problems leading to EMR dissatisfaction, such as information overload, lack of information, and time spent on data entry. As key stakeholders in the successful deployment and utilization of EMRs, physician feedback is essential.

Healthcare administrators should continuously evaluate the benefits of EMRs for physicians and their patients regardless of the level of EMR adoption in their particular organizations.

Furthermore, decision makers need a more comprehensive approach to set HIT priorities and obtain maximum benefits from limited resources, and they must be able to do this without compromising the ethical and social values underpinning their health systems.[6]

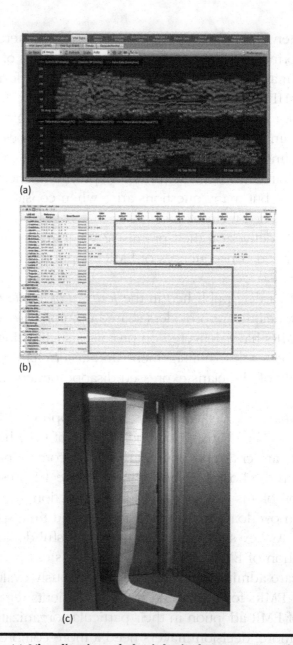

(a)

(b)

(c)

Figure 1.1 **(a) Visualization of physiological parameters within EMR (information overload). (b) Visualization of laboratory parameters in spreadsheet-like EMR (lack of information). (c) Printed-on-paper pre-anesthesia evaluation electronic form (EMR data entry).**

Historical Essay

In the late 1960s, Dr. Larry Weed introduced the concept of the problem-oriented medical record instead of recording diagnoses and their treatment. Multiple parallel efforts then started to develop EMRs. In the mid-1960s, Lockheed created an EMR system that later became Eclipsys (now called Allscripts). This system included computerized physician order entry (CPOE). In 1968, the computer-stored ambulatory record (COSTAR) was developed by Massachusetts General Hospital and Harvard. This system had a modular design separated into accounting and clinical elements. COSTAR was created using the MUMPS programming language, which 40 years later dominates modern EMR suites and financial applications. In 1972, the Regenstrief Institute developed their system, which featured an integration of electronic clinical data from their laboratories and pharmacies. In the 1980s, systems moved from inpatient to outpatient settings. This change was made based on the need for simple billing functions to justify the return on investment for EMRs. Over time, those functions became more dominant than clinical functions. Through the 1990s and 2000s, technical platforms and core systems did not change much. This left clinical functionality far behind the current requirements for safety, efficacy, effectiveness, and usability.

Definitions

Technology is a broad concept that deals with the use and knowledge of tools and crafts and how such use affects people's ability to control and adapt to the social and physical environment.

> *Technology assessment* is a scientific, interactive, and communicative process that aims to contribute to the formation of public and political opinion on societal aspects of science and technology. Technology assessment was (and is) an extremely broad field.

Health technology is defined as the drugs, devices, and medical and surgical procedures used in the prevention, diagnosis, treatment, and rehabilitation of disease.

Assessment is a process of measuring existing technology against claimed goals and objectives.

Health technology assessment is a multidisciplinary activity that systematically examines the safety, clinical efficacy and effectiveness, cost, cost-effectiveness, organizational implications, social consequences, and legal and ethical considerations of the application of a health technology—usually a drug, medical device, or clinical/surgical procedure.

Evaluation is a system of measurement or a set of criteria used to see if an existing technology is working or needs improvement, according to its purpose and objectives.

Research is the systematic process of developing new knowledge by collecting and analyzing data about a particular subject.

What is the difference between evaluation and assessment? Assessment is the process and methodology used to measure technology. Evaluation is a measure of the effectiveness of the assessment.

What is the difference between evaluation and research? Evaluation is used to determine the value and effectiveness of technology within more restricted contexts. Research is used to develop new knowledge of technology within a global perspective or a very specific question.

Health Information Technology (HIT) is the application of information processing that involves both computer hardware and software and that deals with the storage, retrieval, sharing, and use of healthcare information, data, and knowledge for communication and decision making. Technology and HIT is applied science.

History of Technology Assessment

The term *technology assessment* came into use in the 1960s, especially in the United States, and focused on such issues as the implications of supersonic transport, pollution of the environment, and the ethics of genetic screening.[7]

The Office of Technology Assessment (OTA) was an office of the U.S. Congress from 1972 to 1995 with the purpose of providing members of Congress and committees with objective and authoritative analysis of complex scientific and technical issues. OTA was a "leader in practicing and encouraging delivery of public services in innovative and inexpensive ways, including distribution of government documents through electronic publishing."[8] Even though the OTA was permanently closed in 1995, the idea of technology assessment did spread across the world, especially in Europe.

Medical or Health Technology Assessment

In its early years, a health-related technology assessment was called a medical technology assessment (MTA). In the 1980s, the term *health technology assessment* became the dominant term.[7]

HTA has broadened to encompass a wide range of health technologies including drugs, medical devices, medical and surgical procedures, and the organizational and support systems for care provision.[9] The majority of HTAs, however, have been conducted on pharmaceuticals rather than other technologies such as medical devices and surgical procedures.[6] The links between technology assessment and HTA were more or less lost after the dissolution of the OTA, and few workers in the field of HTA seem familiar with the roots of the field in the more general and social-oriented form of assessment.[7]

Health Information Technology Assessment

Recent promises of EMRs to positively impact patients, physicians, and the healthcare system have drawn the attention of society. The field of HIT assessment, however, places grossly disproportionate organization and emphasis on cost-effectiveness.

In 2006, the "Costs and Benefits of Health Information Technology" report was prepared for the United States Agency for Healthcare Research and Quality (AHRQ).[10]

Out of the 256 studies included, no study or collection of studies, outside of those from a handful of HIT leaders, allowed readers to make a determination concerning the generalizable knowledge of the study's reported benefit. Besides the studies from HIT leaders, no other research study comprehensively assessed HIT systems regarding their functionality or included data on costs, relevant information on organizational context and process change, or data on implementation. A small body of literature supports the role of HIT in improving the quality of pediatric care. Also, the ability of EMRs to improve the quality of care in ambulatory care settings was demonstrated in a small series of studies conducted at four sites. Despite the heterogeneity in the analytic methods used, all cost-benefit analyses predicted substantial savings from EHR within a 3–13 year range. The conclusions of the report state that HIT has the potential to enable a dramatic transformation in the delivery of healthcare, making it safer, more effective, and more efficient. Widespread implementation of HIT, however, has been limited by a lack of generalizable knowledge about what types of HIT and implementation methods will improve care and manage costs for specific health organizations.

The need for an unbiased, scientific assessment of HIT using the best possible scientific methods and evidence is clear, and the goal must be to address the questions of clinicians, patients, and decision makers.

1.3 Regulatory Framework in the United States

When discussing new devices or technologies, the government's task is to achieve a balance between innovation, medical progress, safety, and efficiency. After the United States closed the OTA in 1995, many countries in Europe used a wide array of approaches to control the costs of health technology and support the optimal use of such products. HTA has had an increasing role in national health policy development, which has determined the relative value of investment.

Since 1996, the U.S. federal government has taken a number of steps that have affected HIT.

In 2004, President Bush issued Executive Order 13335, which called for the widespread adoption of interoperable EHRs in the next 10 years. He established the Office of the National Coordinator of Health Information Technology (ONC), which required the development and execution of a strategic plan for nationwide implementation of HIT in both the public and private sectors.

The Health Information Technology for Economic and Clinical Health (HITECH) Act directs the ONC to support and promote meaningful use of certified EMR through the adoption of standards and implementation specifications. The Certification Commission for Health Information Technology (CCHIT) is a non profit organization that certified the first EHR products in 2006. In November 2014, the CCHIT stopped certification activity. CCHIT certification was based on the functionality, compatibility, and security of EHR products. From the standpoint of functionality, EHR products need to offer every capability that a doctor needs to manage patients' healthcare in an efficient, high quality, and safe manner in an electronic format. In terms of compatibility, EHR products should meet a base standard for sending and receiving medical data as well as be able to be adapted and updated when necessary. Furthermore, each EHR technology needs the ability to maintain proper security standards.

Since 2015, the ONC has run the Health IT Certification Program, which is performed by ONC-approved accreditors (https://www.healthit.gov/policy-researchers-implementers/about-onc-health-it-certification-program).

CCHIT and ONC certification did not efficiently evaluate the effectiveness or usability of HIT. These were part of the most recent and most significant government initiative surrounding HIT: the American Recovery and Reinvestment Act (ARRA) of 2009. Part of the ARRA is the HITECH Act, which authorizes incentive payments through Medicare and Medicaid to clinicians and hospitals when they use EHRs in a specific way, known as meaningful use.

Food and Drug Administration

For over one hundred years, the Food and Drug Administration (FDA) has been responsible for protecting and promoting public health through the regulation and supervision of food safety, tobacco products, dietary supplements, prescription and over-the-counter pharmaceutical drugs (medications), vaccines, biopharmaceuticals, blood transfusions, medical devices, electromagnetic radiation emitting devices (ERED), and veterinary products.

Some medical software or devices, however, have been marked as "510(k) cleared."

Devices or software are marked "cleared" after being reviewed by the FDA and a premarket notification, in compliance with section 510(k) of the Food, Drug, and Cosmetic Act. For such a device or software to be cleared, it must show that it is "substantially equivalent" to a device that is already legally marketed for the same use.

The evaluation of the efficacy, usability, and impact on patient-centered outcomes of HIT is outside the usual scope of the FDA.

Agency for Healthcare Research and Quality

The mission of the AHRQ is to produce evidence to make healthcare safer, higher quality, more accessible, equitable, and affordable. It is also tasked with working within the U.S. Department of Health and Human Services and with other partners to make sure that evidence is understood and used. The AHRQ conducts and supports studies of the outcomes and effectiveness of diagnostic, therapeutic, and preventive healthcare services and procedures.

The AHRQ does not, however, routinely evaluate HIT efficacy, usability, and impact on patient-centered outcomes.

For a systematic review of the available evidence on health technology, HTA employs a multidisciplinary framework to address four principal questions[11]:

1. Is the technology effective?
2. For whom does the technology work?
3. What costs are entailed in its use?
4. How does the technology compare with available treatment alternatives?

The principal aim of this framework is to provide a range of stakeholders (typically those involved in the funding, planning, purchasing, and investment in healthcare) with accessible, usable, and evidence-based information to guide decisions about the use and diffusion of technology and the efficient allocation of resources.

Other factors are often considered:

■ Necessity (e.g., disease burden and severity)
■ Public health impact
■ Availability of alternative treatments
■ Equity
■ Financial/budget impact

- Projected product utilization
- Innovation of product (e.g., pharmacological characteristics, ease of use)
- Affordability and financial impact

HTA has been called "the bridge between evidence and policy-making," as it provides information for healthcare decision makers at macro-, meso-, and micro-levels.[12]

In this light, and with the widespread use of HIT, evaluation of HIT at the user level is still critical.

During his inaugural address, President Obama mentioned that we will "restore science to its rightful place." The $22 billion invested in science research and development through the ARRA was a first step. Increasing the National Institute of Health's 2016 budget by $2 billion, the biggest boost of the past 12 years, was another positive step. The logical next step, however, is to restore robust science resources for unbiased technical and scientific assessments of medical technologies, especially HIT evaluation focused on clinical outcomes.

1.4 Fundamental Steps Required for Meaningful HIT Evaluation

The introduction of new technology, including computer (informatics) technology, always impacts clinical practice. Appropriately designed and implemented, informatics technologies can help healthcare providers improve clinical workflow, quality of service, care safety, and efficiency. It can also support more effective interactions between patients, families, providers both inside and outside the clinical service, and the whole healthcare organization.

Ultimately, any new HIT intervention should be compared with current practice. The first step is to understand the practice and its needs to maximize the positive impact on technology and minimize the risk of negative effects. The focus of evaluation should be the specific practice that will be most significantly impacted by the new technology.

Limited and inappropriate evaluation are considered the major barriers to moving toward more meaningful HIT advancement, and failure to evaluate the clinical impact of new informatics is a major problem. The top-down approach, engineer/manager-driven development, and little involvement of end users in the process, especially during the design stage, has resulted in expensively developed tools that have been discontinued due to their little impact on actual practice or unanticipated implementation issues.

Evaluation using randomized clinical trials (RCT) may not always be appropriate for informatics systems because the type of questions asked in an informatics evaluation are broader than "hard" clinical and economic outcomes. They are extended to end users' acceptance and patient-oriented outcomes.

A comprehensive evaluation of health informatics tools requires a broader range of research methods, involving both quantitative and qualitative approaches.

There are fundamental differences in defining "standards" in medicine versus standards in industry:

- Industry standards determine whether the equipment or software (technology) can be manufactured to an agreed-upon standard and whether the equipment does what it says it does.
- Clinical standards determine whether what the technology does is important.

The ideal method, or combination of methods, should be determined by the research questions in the context of time

frame and environment. The main criteria for rigorous evaluation can be outlined as follows[13]:

1. Technologic capability: The ability of the technology to
   perform to specifications in a laboratory setting has been
   demonstrated.
2. Range of possible uses: The technology promises to
   provide important information in a range of clinical
   situations.
3. Diagnostic accuracy: The technology provides information
   that allows healthcare workers to make a more accurate assessment regarding the presence and severity of
   disease.
4. Impact on healthcare providers: The technology allows
   healthcare workers to be more confident of their diagnoses, thereby decreasing their anxiety and increasing their
   comfort.
5. Therapeutic impact: The therapeutic decisions made by
   healthcare providers are altered as a result of the application of the technology.
6. Patient outcome: Application of the technology results in
   benefits to the patient.

HIT evaluation is a multidisciplinary field and requires
expertise in at least those fields outlined in Figure 1.2.

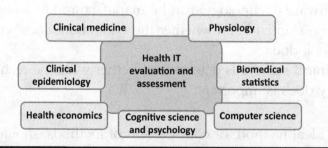

Figure 1.2 Expertise required for HIT evaluation.

Suggested Reading

Scales DC, Laupacis A. Health technology assessment in critical care. *Intensive Care Med.* 2007;33(12):2183–2191. PMID: 17952404.

References

1. HIMSS Analytics. EMR effectiveness: The positive benefit electronic medical record; 2014. http://www.healthcareitnews. com/directory/himss-analytics.
2. Thompson G, O'Horo JC, Pickering BW, Herasevich V. Impact of the electronic medical record on mortality, length of stay, and cost in the hospital and ICU: A systematic review and meta-analysis. *Crit Care Med.* 2015;43(6):1276–1282.
3. Jonsson E, Banta D. Treatments that fail to prove their worth: Interview by Judy Jones. *BMJ.* 1999;319(7220):1293.
4. Lawrence G. Tobacco smoke enemas. *Lancet.* 2002;359(9315):1442.
5. Terry K. EHRs' broken promise: What must be done to win back your trust. *Medical Economics.* 2015. http://medicaleconomics.modernmedicine.com/medical-economics/news/ehrs-broken-promise. Accessed November 12, 2015.
6. Hutton J, McGrath C, Frybourg J-M, Tremblay M, Bramley-Harker E, Henshall C. Framework for describing and classifying decision-making systems using technology assessment to determine the reimbursement of health technologies (fourth hurdle systems). *Int J Technol Assess Health Care.* 2006;22(1):10–18.
7. Banta D. What is technology assessment? *Int J Technol Assess Health Care.* 2009;25(Suppl 1):7–9.
8. Nancy K, Kubasek GSS. *Environmental Law.* 6th edn. Upper Saddle River, NJ: Prentice Hall; 2007. http://www.amazon.com/ gp/product/0136142168?keywords=9780136142164&qid=1450059 677&ref_=sr_1_2&sr=8-2. Accessed December 14, 2015.
9. Jonsson E. Development of health technology assessment in Europe: A personal perspective. *Int J Technol Assess Health Care.* 2002;18(2):171–183. http://www.ncbi.nlm.nih.gov/ pubmed/12053417.

10. Shekelle PG, Morton SC, Keeler EB. *Costs and Benefits of Health Information Technology*. Evidence Report/Technology Assessment No. 13 2. (Prepared by the Southern California Evidence-based Practice Center under Contract No. 290-02-0003.) AHRQ Publication No. 06-E006.
11. Sorenson C, Drummond M, Kanavos P. *Ensuring Value for Money in Health Care, The Role of Health Technology Assessment in the European Union*. Copenhagen: WHO Regional Office Europe; 2008.
12. Battista RN, Hodge MJ. The evolving paradigm of health technology assessment: Reflections for the millennium. *CMAJ*. 1999;160(10):1464–1467. http://www.ncbi.nlm.nih.gov/pubmed/10352637.
13. Guyatt GH, Tugwell PX, Feeny DH, Haynes RB, Drummond M. A framework for clinical evaluation of diagnostic technologies. *CMAJ*. 1986;134(6):587–594. http://www.ncbi.nlm.nih.gov/pubmed/3512062.

Chapter 2

Structure and Design of Evaluation Studies

2.1 Review of Study Methodologies and Approaches That Can Be Used in Health IT Evaluations

The overall goal of healthcare information technology (HIT or health IT) evaluations is to provide feedback information to decision makers, clinicians, administrators, patients, and other relevant people and groups. This is the fundamental difference between scientific investigation and scientific evaluation. We need to receive definite answers to specific questions. One of the major goals of evaluation is to influence decision making through information.

General steps in informatics evaluations may be outlined as follows:

1. Define the health IT (application, system) to be studied.
2. Define the stakeholders whose questions should be addressed.
3. Define and prioritize study questions.

4. Choose the appropriate methodology to minimize bias and address generalizability (Chapter 3).
5. Select reliable, valid measurement methods (Chapter 4).
6. Carry out the study.
7. Prepare publication for results dissemination (report, press release, publication in scientific journal) (Chapter 5).

Define the Health IT (Application, System) to Be Studied

Modern software applications range from simple, single-purpose mobile apps to large, complex electronic health records (EHRs) systems interacting with multiple external systems. From the very beginning, the evaluator should define very clearly what system or element of the system will be studied. A complex system may be evaluated as a whole for some high-level impact metrics; however, to evaluate specific effects, an appropriate part of a large system should be isolated and studied. Single-purpose applications exist to carry out very focused objectives. The impact of these metrics needs to be evaluated. At this stage, feasibility should be taken into account, and consultation with colleagues and experienced members of the team is important. Timing of the study itself and calculation of the sample size for active project time estimation are additional important variables to use.

Define the Stakeholders Whose Questions Should Be Addressed

Given the growing use of mobile medical apps in addition to healthcare institution–based software, there is a need to address all stakeholders' questions, not only the implementation or purchase questions of decision makers. That is the main difference between classical technology assessment and modern health IT evaluation.

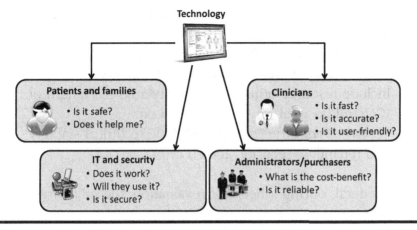

Figure 2.1 Health IT evaluation stakeholders and the questions they ask. (Modified from Friedman and Wyatt, 1997.)

The primary users of health technologies are clinical providers, patients, and patients' families. Another group is information technology (IT) personnel (including security) and administrators (purchasers). It is obvious that all these groups will have different demands for technology utilities and will ask different questions for evaluation purposes (Figure 2.1).

Define and Prioritize Study Questions

Questions that matter most to patients and clinicians may be called "clinically oriented outcomes of interest" and are organized in the following two major domains:

1. *Better health (clinical outcome measurements)*: Examples include rate of intensive care unit (ICU)-acquired complications, discharge home, hospital mortality, ICU and hospital readmission, and so on.
2. *Better care (clinical process measurements)*: Examples include adherence to and appropriateness of processes of care, provider satisfaction, provider adoption, patient attitudes, and so on.

The following two domains would be secondary from the perspective of those groups but are primary for administrators and IT:

3. *Lower cost (financial impact measurements)*: Examples include resource utilization, severity-adjusted length of ICU and hospital stay, cost, and so on.
4. *Technical validity*: Examples include technical stability and reliability, security, and so on.

In general, during a health IT evaluation, the following four questions must be answered:

1. Is the technology safe?
2. Does the technology do what it is supposed to do?
3. Is what technology does useful?
4. Can the technology be applied to my practice?

These components can be organized in a framework for diagnostic and therapeutic health IT evaluation (Figure 2.2).

Individuals have a tendency to trust numbers rather than statements. But qualitative studies add another dimension to the HIT evaluation process, helping stakeholders and

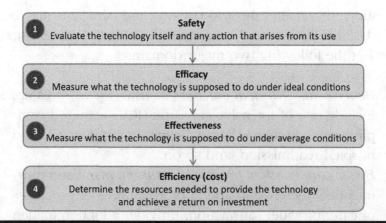

Figure 2.2 Components as steps for a clinically meaningful HIT evaluation.

facilitating an understanding of how users interact with systems. The results are also helpful for communicating with a larger general audience.

Quantitative studies: Objective measurement is used—quantitative variables that are clearly defined and directly obtained.

Qualitative studies: Subjective measurement is a qualitative approach that is based on opinions or judgments related to human responses to actual or potential study questions. The purpose of qualitative studies is to describe, explore, and explain the topic studied. As qualitative measurements, lessons learned are important outcome measures. These may describe organizational, financial, legal, or technical barriers that the project encounters. Facilitators may be leadership support, seamless training, and user buy-in. To capture these metrics, meetings with the study team and users to openly discuss the issues are crucial. Focus groups with targeted individuals can help to capture information more formally. Audio recording is helpful for future transcripts and analysis.

2.2 Clinical Research Design Overview

All aspects of a study design and analysis are based on the aims and objectives of the study. It is very important that all elements of the study are documented in the study's protocol and written precisely. This, in particular, serves two objectives: support of the process of evaluation to generate answers to specific questions and use of that information for audit and post hoc assessment by stakeholders. Another important role of the study protocol is the foundation and supply details for future publications. After defining the study objectives (aims), the next step is the choice of an appropriate research study design. To measure the real live impact of technology, the first step is usually a before-after study or a randomized controlled trial (RCT).

An RCT is the most powerful experimental design; however, in most situations, it is not feasible or ethical to perform a study of technologies on live human subjects. Also, the questions that can be answered by studies utilizing the RCT design are limited and cannot address all the concerns of robust evaluations.

Before-after experiments have been shown to be prone to influence by biases and confounders that lead to invalid conclusions and may result in incorrect understanding of the system under study.

Choosing the appropriate study methodology is a crucial step in health IT evaluation. Clinical epidemiology methodology also plays an essential role.

Clinical Epidemiology Evidence Pyramid

An important concept in clinical epidemiology and evidence-based medicine (EBM) that should be used for evaluating health IT for clinically meaningful outcomes is the EBM pyramid. The EBM pyramid is a conceptually simple diagram that explains how to differentiate levels of evidence and study design based on the relative strengths and weaknesses that influence health-related decisions (Figure 2.3).

Systematic reviews focus on a particular clinical topic and are based on a literature search that is carried out according to the specific methodology conducted to identify studies with sound methodologies. After assessing studies for inclusion and exclusion criteria and quality, the results are summarized according to review questions. In the area of health IT, there are a limited number of such publications due to an insufficient number of studies; weak, biased methodology; or heterogeneity.[1,2] This method is useful for high-level decisions, for new technology design, and with sufficient evidence, for individual technology applicability.

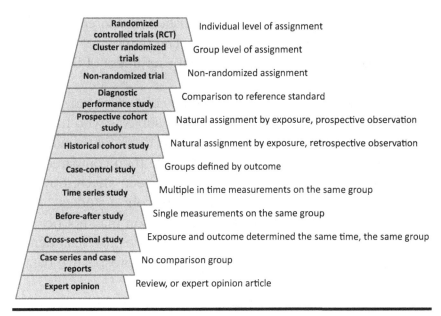

Figure 2.3 EBM pyramid. Study designs and some characteristics. The lower level in the pyramid has lower evidence to support conclusions.

Randomized controlled trials are carefully planned experiments that use intervention (treatment or exposure) to study its effect on real live subjects and can provide sound evidence of cause and effect. Methodology can reduce the potential for bias (randomization and blinding) that allows for comparison between intervention groups and control (no intervention) groups. There are multiple variations of parallel group designs (e.g., crossover, stepped wedge) that may be more feasible in particular situations. Often, RCTs are impossible to use for health IT evaluations, as randomization intervention may be costly, time consuming, unethical, and infeasible to use. Blinding is often also impossible to use within technology interventions. Randomization could be successfully used in laboratory-based studies (safe environment).

Diagnostic performance studies show the efficacy of a new test (alert) compared to an established measurement. It is an experiment when a new test under investigation is compared to the gold standard (established measurement) on the same subjects in the study group. The number of measurements helps to determine the potential usefulness of the new intervention.

Cohort studies could be considered as observational "natural experiment" studies. A group of subjects who have already undergone or have been exposed to an intervention are followed over time. Their outcomes are then compared with those of a similar group that has not been affected by or exposed to the studied intervention. In cohort studies, groups may be different, and then comparison may not be reliable. Historical (retrospective) cohort studies use data that have been collected in the past compared to prospective data collection.

Case-control studies are studies in which the outcome of interest (condition) is already known. That group of subjects or patients is compared with another group who do not have that outcome. The scientist looks back to identify factors or exposures that might be associated with the outcomes of interest. This process often relies on databases or human ability to recall past information. The biggest problem with studies behind multiple biases is that the statistical relationship (association) does not mean that one factor necessarily caused the other (causation).

Cross-sectional (descriptive) studies describe the relationship between the outcome of interest and other factors at one point in time in a defined group. These studies are lacking in relationship timing information between intervention/exposure and outcome.

Case series and case reports are collections of reports on the specific intervention results and can describe group or individual cases. Because they only report intervention cases and use no control groups to compare outcomes, they have little statistical validity.

Study designs should be used based on technology type, the characteristics of the target population, and the specific question asked. Also, the feasibility and ethical aspects need to be considered. Experimental study designs such as RCT are powerful tools and can be used in areas of health IT to obtain evidence on systems' impacts. Quasi-experimental designs are the second-best choice when an experiment cannot be done. Nonexperimental observational studies with control groups may be useful, but biases could completely change the picture. Involvement by a content expert and end statistician can help minimize the impact of bias. Nonexperimental studies without control groups can be considered as a starting point; however, they do not provide sufficient evidence to support conclusions and are not adequate for decision making (Figure 2.4).

The protocol and final report should describe the study design for goals to be evaluated by the readership and provide the ability to reproduce the study.

Specific Study Design Considerations in Health IT Evaluation

Health IT "products" are organized around informatics technologies and, as subjects, could be represented with hardware, software, or a combination of both. This could predefine study locations that could be done virtually in three locations:

1. Virtual setting: Computerized environment completely isolated from laboratory and field. Used in the study of the development of health IT products, and in evaluation, could be used in efficiency (cost) studies. Access to a number of databases and information sources is required, but access to patients or providers is not needed. Some usability studies could be done in a virtual environment if done by a developer or researcher.
2. Laboratory setting: Isolated from the real clinical care environment and field setting. The laboratory may or may not have feeds and access to real health IT products such

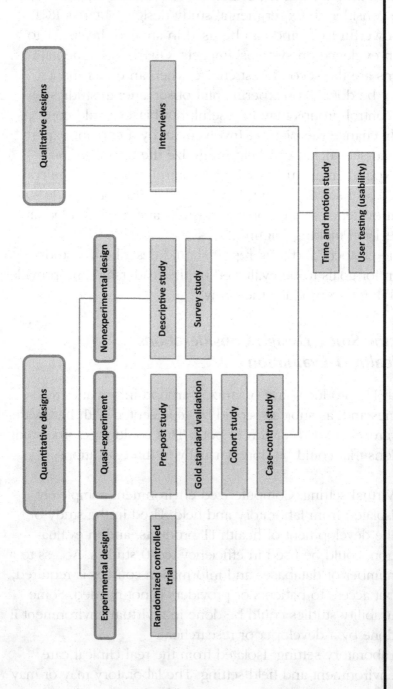

Figure 2.4 Typical study designs useful for health IT evaluation.

as EMR. None of the study procedures affect patient care and provider duties. The laboratory setting is the basis for efficacy studies that measure the impact of technology under ideal conditions. The majority of usability studies require access to a laboratory.
3. Field setting: "Live" environment when the studied technology is used in real clinical care and affects patients. This setting is the basis for effectiveness studies and also could be used for some usability studies.

Randomized Controlled Trial in Health IT

An RCT is considered the gold standard in studying the impact of interventions, such as medications, but it has significant limitations for wide adoption in HIT evaluations.

One of the main reasons is its very high cost. Done correctly, it is a costly type of study. In the world of the pharmaceutical industry, a placebo-controlled, double-blind RCT is the study design of choice for support evidence to the Food and Drug Administration (FDA) for market approval of new drugs. As, currently, there is no requirement for FDA approval of EMR or a majority of software health IT products, this study design is not popular within the industry.

However, because an RCT is considered the strongest study design in the evidence pyramid, researchers should consider such a design for use in field setting evaluations. The following items should be considered as pertinent for technology:

■ Due to the nature of technological intervention, it is almost impossible to do a blind study. Subjects are almost always aware of the technology that they use.
■ Inferiority (placebo) and noninferiority (equivalence) trials. Sometimes, it is impossible or nonethical to compare a studied intervention with nontreatment (placebo). In this situation, a comparison using the best available practice could be a solution. An example of an equivalence trial

would be a new EMR module in addition to the current
EMR compared to practices that use the current EMR
without the new EMR module.

■ Crossover and cluster randomized trial.[3] Sometimes, it is
impossible to do individual patient or provider randomization to technology due to technical, administrative,
workflow, or ethical issues. In this situation, crossover
randomization or stepped-wedge cluster randomization
may be an alternative. Figure 2.5 explains the intervention schedule for such trials. Crossover trials may be difficult to perform in situations in which users adopt and
like technology during the intervention phase. It would
be very dissatisfactory to withdraw an intervention after
successful implementation. Stepped-wedge cluster randomized trials could be successfully used to avoid the
pitfalls of parallel and crossover trials. The time sequence

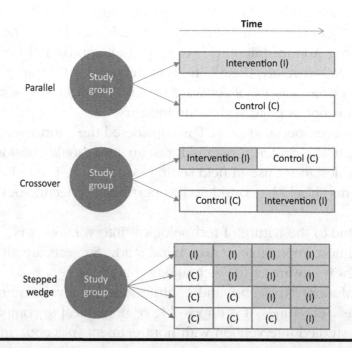

**Figure 2.5   Time sequence of parallel, crossover, and stepped-wedge
randomized trials in terms of intervention and control groups.**

of three major randomized trial designs is outlined in Figure 2.5.

Diagnostic Performance Study

Establishing a diagnosis is not an absolute process and is based on probability rather than certainty. There is always the possibility of false results compared to a true diagnosis. In health IT, this concept is applied for any kind of alert or notification system evaluation. For a system to be useful in a real live application, it should be compared to the gold standard or reference standard.

This metric is important in particular for the evaluation of decision support systems based on notification mechanisms (alerts or "sniffers") because false positive alerts trigger the same actions as true positive. Also with the high rate of false negative tests, users miss events and quickly lose trust in the system.

More details on the statistics that should be calculated for a diagnostic performance study are provided in Chapter 4.

2.3 How to Ask Good Evaluation Questions and Develop Protocol

Good evaluation questions for clinically relevant problems should always be designed around the PICO concept. This is the first step to formulating good, answerable questions.

- *Patient, population, or problem*: What is the patient or population of interest? Subgroups? Setting?
- *Intervention (or exposure)*: What do you do with the patient? What is the intervention of interest? Device, software? Time frame?
- *Comparison*: What is the alternative to intervention to be compared? Another technology? No technology?

■ *Outcome*: What is the relevant outcome of interest and end point? Mortality? Complications?

As a step in the preparation of a strong evaluation protocol, research and synthesize current knowledge and scientific evidence. This information should be written as a part of the background and rationale. All aspects, including negative information, should be described. This becomes part of the limitation section of the proposal, the protocol, and later, the report/manuscript (Table 2.1).

The following is a summary of the general recommendations by Ammenwerth et al.[4]

1. Evaluation takes time; thus, take enough time for thorough planning and execution.
2. Document all of your decisions and steps in a detailed study protocol. Adhere to this protocol; it is your main tool for a systematic evaluation.
3. Strive for management support, and try to organize long-term financial support.
4. Clarify the goals of the evaluation. Take into account the different stakeholder groups. Resolve conflicting goals.
5. Reduce your evaluation questions to an appropriate number of the most important questions that you can handle within the available time and budget. If new questions emerge during the study that cannot be easily integrated, postpone them for a new evaluation study.
6. Clarify and thoroughly describe the IT and the environment that are the object of your evaluation. Take note of any changes in the IT and its environment during the study that may affect results.
7. Select an adequate study design. Think of a stepwise study design.
8. Select adequate methods to answer your study questions. Neither objectivist nor subjectivist approaches can answer all questions. Take into account the available methods.

Table 2.1 Summary of Study Characteristics for Major Types of Evaluation Studies

Type	Broad Study Question	Stakeholders	Version of Technology	Study Subjects	Study Tasks	Study Setting	Study Objects
Safety evaluation	Is technology safe?	Funders, certification agencies	Prototype or release	Patients, users	Simulation, real	Laboratory, field	Quality, methods
Efficacy	Is technology functioning as intended?	Developers, certification agencies	Prototype or release	Users	Simulation	Laboratory	Quality, components, structure
Effectiveness	Does technology have the potential to be beneficial in the real world?	Developers, users	Prototype or release	Patients, users	Real	Field	Tasks completion, speed, user comments

(Continued)

Table 2.1 (Continued)   Summary of Study Characteristics for Major Types of Evaluation Studies

Type	Broad Study Question	Stakeholders	Version of Technology	Study Subjects	Study Tasks	Study Setting	Study Objects
Efficiency (cost)	Does technology have the potential to be beneficial?	Developers, funders, academic community	None, prototype or release	None	None, real	Virtual	Accuracy, speed
Usability	Can user navigate and carry out intended function?	Developers, funders, users	Prototype or release	Patients, users	Simulation, real	Laboratory, field	Accuracy, speed

Consider being multimethodic and multidisciplinary, and consider the triangulation of methods, data sources, investigators, and theories. Strive for methodical (e.g., biometrics) advice.

9. Motivate a sufficient number of users to participate. Consider multicentric trials and financial or other compensation.
10. Use validated evaluation instruments whenever possible.
11. Be open to unwanted and unexpected effects.
12. Publish your results and what you learned to allow others to learn from your work.

Suggested Reading

Article with practical advice for better protocol: Guyatt G. Preparing a research protocol to improve chances for success. *J Clin Epidemiol.* 2006 Sep;59(9):893–899. PMID: 16895810.

Chrzanowski RS, Paccaud F. Study design for technology assessment: Critical issues. *Health Policy.* 1988;9(3):285–296. http://www.ncbi.nlm.nih.gov/pubmed/10302542.

Clarke K, O'Moore R, Smeets R, et al. A methodology for evaluation of knowledge-based systems in medicine. *Artif Intell Med.* 1994;6(2):107–121. http://www.ncbi.nlm.nih.gov/pubmed/8049752.

Cusack CM, Byrne C, Hook JM, McGowan J, Poon EG, Zafar A. Health information technology evaluation toolkit: 2009 update. (Prepared for the AHRQ National Resource Center for Health Information Technology under Contract No. 290-04-0016.) AHRQ Publication No. 09-0083-EF. Rockville, MD: Agency for Healthcare Research and Quality; June 2009.

Friedman CP, Wyatt JC. *Evaluation Methods in Medical Informatics. Computers and Medicine.* New York: Springer, 1997.

Goodman CS. *HTA 101: Introduction to Health Technology Assessment.* Bethesda, MD: National Library of Medicine (US); 2014. Direct PDF link (218pp): https://www.nlm.nih.gov/nichsr/hta101/HTA_101_FINAL_7-23-14.pdf.

Guyatt GH, Tugwell PX, Feeny DH, Haynes RB, Drummond M. A framework for clinical evaluation of diagnostic technologies. *CMAJ*. 1986;134(6):587–594. http://www.ncbi.nlm.nih.gov/pubmed/3512062.

Health Services Research Information Central. Evidence-based practice and health technology assessment: https://www.nlm.nih.gov/hsrinfo/evidence_based_practice.html.

References

1. Thompson G, O'Horo JC, Pickering BW, Herasevich V. Impact of the electronic medical record on mortality, length of stay, and cost in the hospital and ICU: A systematic review and metaanalysis. *Crit Care Med*. 2015;43(6):1276–1282.
2. Kashiouris M, O'Horo JC, Pickering BW, Herasevich V. Diagnostic performance of electronic syndromic surveillance systems in acute care: A systematic review. *Appl Clin Inform*. 2013;4:212–224.
3. Hussey MA, Hughes JP. Design and analysis of stepped wedge cluster randomized trials. *Contemp Clin Trials*. 2007;28(2):182–191.
4. Ammenwerth E, Gräber S, Herrmann G, Bürkle T, König J. Evaluation of health information systems: Problems and challenges. *Int J Med Inform*. 2003;71(2–3):125–135. http://www.ncbi.nlm.nih.gov/pubmed/14519405.

Chapter 3

Study Design and Measurements Fundamentals

The main goal of an evaluation study and related measurements is to establish the true relationship between intervention and outcome. This relationship should be measured statistically and the results should be valid. To be able to do this, the investigator/evaluator should use appropriate measurement techniques. Statistics in a broad sense are mathematical tools. Even if correctly executed, without appropriately addressing clinical epidemiology principles, statistical results may not be valid. The classical illustration of this problem is shown in Figure 3.1. Applied to two independent measurements, the statistics show perfect correlation >99%; however, it is obvious that one of those measurements does not cause the other.

Causal inference is a big problem within the growing field of "big data" and the data science profession. Since multiple factors contribute to final conclusions, it is extremely important to understand and deal with those factors (Figure 3.2).

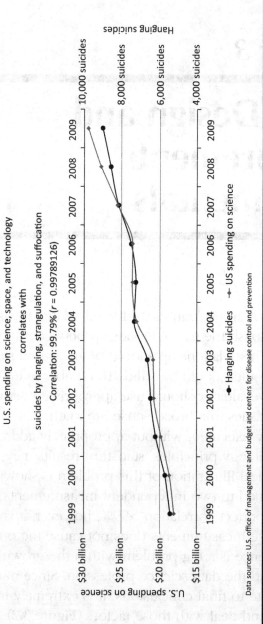

Figure 3.1 Correlation is not causation. (From http://www.tylervigen.com/spurious-correlations [Creative Common 4 license].)

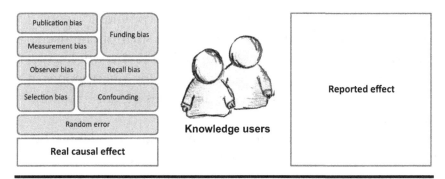

Figure 3.2   Factors contributing to the difference between the real causal effect ("truth") and the reported effect.

To be able to perform methodologically correct evaluation studies, evaluators should understand basic epidemiological principles and apply them at the protocol development stage.

3.1 Fundamental Principles of Study Design

Selection Criteria and Sample

Population is described as a complete set of people in a defined area. Usually, it is used as a geographic, demographic, and temporal term. It is obvious that a study targeted in healthcare information technology (HIT or health IT) cannot be done on the whole population, since some people are not concerned about technology at all. A *target population* is a smaller set of the people who use technology (e.g., mobile phone users). However, for a number of reasons, the entire target population is impossible to recruit into a study.

An *accessible population* is a subset of the target population who potentially could be included in a study. On the other hand, a *study sample* is a subset of the accessible population who participates in a study.

The challenge lies in choosing a study sample so that the result of the study could be applied (generalizability) to the entire target population. For example, if you are studying a mobile application for tracking health in a community, your study sample should include young, active smartphone users. The results of this study cannot be applied to the whole city, since the elderly population may not be using smartphones at all, or if they do, they are having difficulties because the font in the application is small.

The first fundamental step in study design is to define the target population and analyze the sample to see if it serves the study question appropriately.

Selection criteria: Determine what a study sample looks like.

Inclusion criteria: Define the relevant group that should be included in the study. Selection criteria address if temporal and geographic (administrative) location could be used as a trade-off between scientific and practical goals. Inclusion criteria should be defined by the following dimensions:

1. Demographic characteristics: Age, race, sex, and social and economic characteristics.
2. Clinical characteristics: Specific condition or disease of patients.
3. Geographic or administrative characteristics: Specific location or study area.
4. Temporal characteristics: Time when the study was performed. Sample size estimation affects this factor.

Exclusion criteria define what might interfere with the success of the study. For interventional studies, the safety of the participants should be considered.

There are many exclusion criteria that should be addressed in the methodology part of the evaluation protocol. There may be subjects who (1) are at risk of harm or adverse effects, (2) cannot provide reliable data, or (3) are likely to not complete the study or be lost to follow-up.

The general rule is to have the fewest possible exclusion criteria and keep enrolment simple. There is no single recipe on how to choose the inclusion and exclusion criteria. However, strict limitation introduces selection bias, which could be addressed in the resulting publication.

If the number of subjects who meet the selection criteria is large, researchers should choose a subset (sample) for the study. The best sampling technique is random sampling, but in health science research, a random sample of the target population is almost impossible. Often, determination is based on the population that can be easily accessed by the evaluators. That is called a convenience sample. It is a good choice for many researchers and has advantages in terms of cost and logistics. Any sampling technique requires you to make a decision: will conclusions from a sample be similar to those that result from a target population? The sample should represent the whole population.

Validity

As the evaluator proceeds with measurements selection, the important question will be validity: how well does the measurement represent the true measurement of interest? Understanding validity helps in choosing the appropriate methodological designs and interpreting the results.

Validity could be defined in several ways. The following are the main definitions:

1. Internal validity: Does the intervention/observation work in a defined population (study sample)? Inference from subjects should be accurate and should avoid systematic errors or bias.
2. External validity: Is defined by results generalizability—to what populations, settings, and conditions the observed effect can be applied. External validity is important for any large decision making on technology or broader implementation. An inappropriate extrapolation finding to a broader setting could not only be useless but also dangerous.

3. Face validity: The ability of a measure to reasonably represent a concept as judged by a domain expert.
4. Content validity: Describes how well a measurement represents all aspects of the true phenomena under study. Outcome measure is often chosen as a marker or surrogate for the real outcome, and content validity describes how well it fits.
5. Construct validity: Defines how well a measurement conforms to theoretical knowledge. It refers to whether the used definition of a variable actually reflects the true theoretical meaning of a concept.
6. Criterion-related validity: Is defined as the degree to which a new measurement correlates with well-accepted existing measures.

The common approach to have a valid measurement is to use literature and expert knowledge to find a good measurement instrument. If there is no available instrument, the evaluator may develop a new instrument and validate it first.

Accuracy and Precision

The best health IT evaluation study should capture the causal effect of interest with minimal error. The major goal of HIT evaluation research is to explain the patterns of outcome and informatics intervention. However, causal effect can be affected by random and systematic errors (Figure 3.3).

Precision is a function of random error. Greater error makes a less precise measurement and influences the power of the study. Precision is a degree of how measurement is reproduced from one measurement to another. There are three main sources of random error: observer, instrument, and subject. Precision could be evaluated for categorical variables by kappa statistic and for continuous variables by the Bland–Altman plot. Correlation should be avoided for this purpose.

For each measurement in the study, the evaluator needs to check and apply strategies to increase precision, such as using

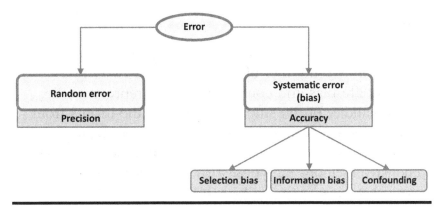

Figure 3.3   Major errors in observational studies.

the standard measurement method, training observers and staff, automating the measurement instrument, refining the measurement instrument, and performing repetitive measurements.

Accuracy is a variable that represents what it intends to represent. Accuracy is a function of systematic error or bias. A less-biased study increases the validity of conclusions. There are three main sources of bias: observer, instrument, and subject. Accuracy should be evaluated and compared with the accurate reference standard, which is often called the "gold standard." Accuracy could be evaluated using the Bland–Altman plot for continuous variables and the diagnostic performance study (sensitivity, specificity) for categorical variables described in Chapter 4.

Classical explanations of accuracy and precision are outlined in Figure 3.4.

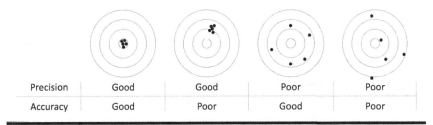

Precision	Good	Good	Poor	Poor
Accuracy	Good	Poor	Good	Poor

Figure 3.4   Relationship and difference between accuracy and precision. The major characteristic to spot the difference between random and systematic errors is their effect on increasing study size; systematic error does not change, but random error magnitude decreases.

Bias

The relationship between intervention and outcome could be affected by a number of factors, and the two most important are bias and confounding. Bias represents the internal validity of the study and deviates the results from the truth. All observational studies have some degree of bias. There are different classifications, and the most comprehensive includes 35 types.[1] However, there are three major categories: selection bias, information bias, and confounding.

Selection bias, in broad terms, could be described as the difference between studied groups. For example, users and non-users of wearable technology that tracks exercises. They could have different socioeconomic status and different motivations to exercise. There may be a difference in age since younger people tend to use technologies more. When we compare the groups of users who use this wearable technology and those who don't, the difference in clinically meaningful outcome (rate of myocardial infarction [MI]) will be significant. The wrong, biased conclusion will be that the use of wearable devices can prevent MI. That is particularly true in this case, but the size of the effect will be grossly overestimated since selection bias was not taken into statistical analysis. Other common types of selection bias include referral, participation, prevalence-incidence, admission rate, non-response, and volunteer bias.

Information (or measurement) *bias* results from the incorrect determination of exposure and/or outcome. Overall, to minimize information bias, better measurement techniques and tools should be used. The common types of information bias include recall, exposure suspicion, diagnostic suspicion, and others.

A separate artifact is the *Hawthorne effect*. This is a tendency of people to perform better when they know that they are under observation. This can significantly change the results of the evaluation.

Confounding

This factor of the variable correlates directly and indirectly with both intervention and outcome. Knowing confounding factors in a specific evaluation project will allow controlling them. One of the control methods is statistical adjustment for confounding variables. Figure 3.5 explains the relationship between baseline state, outcome, intervention, and confounders.

Figure 3.6 explains the principles of dealing with systematic and random errors as the researcher and user of the evaluation report.

Measurement Variables

Measurements are an essential part of evaluation. One type of variable can be more informative than others. There

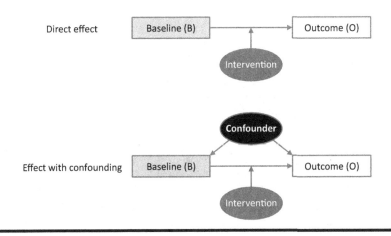

Figure 3.5 Effect of confounding on the outcome. Confounding could be controlled by matching, restriction or stratification, and propensity score. The multivariate statistical technique would also be helpful for controlling biases and confounding variables.

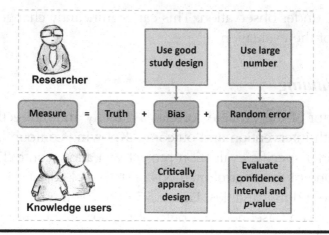

Figure 3.6 Fundamental formula to deal with systematic and random errors from the perspective of researcher and knowledge users.

are simple classifications that are important to understand (Figure 3.7). The type of measurement is used to choose the appropriate statistical test. There are two big groups of variables: continuous and categorical.

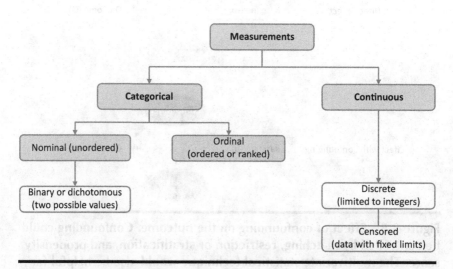

Figure 3.7 Classification of type of data and measurements.

Continuous variables in theory could be measured so accurately that there would be no gaps between possible values (continuum of values).

Categorical variables can be put into a countable number of categories or different groups. They can be further divided into two main subcategories.

Nominal variables have two or more categories but do not have order.

Ordinal variables have two or more categories but can be ordered or ranked.

Dichotomous variables are nominal variables that only have two categories or levels.

The best practice is to use continuous variables as much as possible. They contain more information and result in more statistical power and a smaller sample size. Even if categorical variables are more appropriate to report, continuous variables are better to collect to have more analytic opportunities and then convert as needed.

As a part of the evaluation protocol, a standard operating procedures (SOP) manual should be written. It describes the methods for conducting and recording all measurements in the study.

3.2 Core Measurements in HIT Evaluation

Outcome measurements in health IT evaluation studies involve multiple dimensions and stakeholders (clinician, patient, administration, developers, security, and academic) with the ultimate goal of producing evidence for decision making. They are also dependent on the available resources, time line, and aim of the study.

On the national level, the Joint Commission on Accreditation of Healthcare Organizations (JCAHO) developed performance measurements for healthcare organizations embedded in the accreditation process. Those metrics are important for the process of care evaluation.

As we defined, four stakeholder groups and related questions for HIT evaluation outcome measurements could be divided into the following categories:

1. Better health (clinical outcome measurements)
2. Better care (clinical process measurements)
3. Lower cost (financial impact measurements)

Clinical outcomes are an important category that needs to be an absolute target for most patient-oriented technologies.

Clinical Outcome Measures

Health outcomes are the primary interests in clinical medicine and patients' primary concerns, and can be named as death, disability, and symptoms. These are events that physicians try to predict and change. Clinical outcomes can be grouped into five important domains:

1. Death: Ultimate bad outcome.
2. Disease: Chronic or acute illness with abnormalities and symptoms.
3. Disability: Impaired ability to perform usual daily tasks.
4. Discomfort: Syndromes that make patient uncomfortable.
5. Dissatisfaction: Emotional reaction to illness and care.

Clinical Process Measurements

Outcome measurements track the quality of provided care. These measures use end points associated with high-quality care or relate to long-term goals for quality healthcare. Clinical process measurements could address many aspects of patient care, including the following:

1. Clinical process measures: Efficient use of healthcare resources.
2. Provider adoption and attitude measures: Care coordination.
3. Patient adoption, knowledge, and attitude measures: Patient engagements.
4. Workflow impact measures: Adherence to clinical guidelines.
5. Patient safety.

The usability evaluation of HIT falls under this category, since it has a direct implication on the clinical process, such as adoption and satisfaction. Translating better usability as a direct factor to clinical outcomes is difficult and in most situations not feasible.

Financial Impact Measures

Clinical process outcomes represent the providers' and patients' interests, but financial impact outcomes, including measures of health resource utilization, represent the stakeholders, such as the administrators/payers and HIT vendors. Cost and cost-effectiveness are often excluded from clinical studies; however, these measures are important to understand the whole impact of technology.

There are generally two approaches to measure financial impact. Macro-level measures often evaluate performance on the institution level as whole. Usually, it is a retrospective summary of findings. Results are mostly in the interest of external stakeholders. Micro-level measures focus on the performance of a specific effort or work unit, with usually prospective evaluation. Results are in the interest of local stakeholders and are used as motivation for change or implementation.

1. *Monetary costs*: The most desirable study would be one that examines the direct costs (the monetary costs) of intervention. It also may include measures of indirect costs (e.g., the costs of disability). Often, multiple measures of costs are included in studies.
2. *Health resource utilization*: Measures of health resource utilization, such as the number of outpatient visits, days of hospitalization, or number of days treated with a specific medication, are often used as efficient and easily interpretable proxies for measuring cost. These are helpful in situations when the actual cost is difficult to obtain, and are dependent on numerous factors.

Research questions addressing the issues of cost may be formulated in a number of ways.

Cost minimization studies measure the cost of applying a specific technology to a study population. There are no comparisons to alternative interventions. These studies describe the costs of care for a particular population or the cost of care for a specific condition. This latter approach often requires adjustment to other factors related to care, intervention, and baseline characteristics.

Cost-benefit studies are typically measured in monetary currency. These studies compare the costs of a technological intervention with the standard of care without the studied technology. The outcome is cost savings that result from the benefits of improved treatment.

Cost-effectiveness studies are studies that compare the costs of the impacts and benefits of a specific intervention in terms of a specified, mostly patient-oriented outcome, such as a decrease in mortality, complications, or years of life saved.

Cost evaluation techniques will be described in Chapter 7. Robust health IT evaluation should use a variety of health and economic outcome measures.

Other Outcome Measurement Concepts

The choice of outcome variable depends on the technology involved and the type of study and analysis. Intermediate and composite measures are generally accepted if it is not feasible to get "hard" outcome data. Using such variables requires a strong and scientifically based association between the intermediate effect and the "hard" outcome.

Intermediate Outcome

Intermediate outcome is often a biological marker for the condition of interest. The intention is to use it often to decrease the follow-up period for evaluating the impact of study intervention. An example would be measuring the blood glucose level rather than measuring the effectiveness of the diabetes treatment as a clinical outcome. Reducing the time of the study has its own advantages.

Composite Outcome

Composite outcome is a combination of clinical events that could be extrapolated to clinical outcome. Often, it is a combination of individual elements of the score or combination. Composite outcome increases the power of the study as it occurs more frequently. However, it is sometimes difficult to interpret, replicate in other studies, and compare.

Patient-Reported Outcomes

Patient-reported outcome (PRO) includes any outcome that is based on information provided by patients or by people who can report on their behalf (proxies). It is the patients' rating of their health status, symptoms, functioning, quality of life, and satisfaction with care. Patients could be a good source of information about clinical outcomes or healthcare costs when other sources are unavailable or unreliable.

Health-Related Quality of Life

Health-related quality of life (HRQOL) is a broad, multidimensional concept that usually includes self-reported measures of physical and mental health and social role functioning. HRQOL is defined as "the capacity to perform the usual daily activities for a person's age and major social role."[2] This is usually a subjective composite outcome from the perspective of patients or proxies. This is part of the PRO as a broad concept.

Subjective and Objective Measurements

Clinical outcomes including diagnoses are conclusions based on the assessments of physicians and other clinicians. They are recorded as free text and further coded for administrative and billing purposes using code systems such as the International Classification of Diseases (ICD), Current Procedural Terminology (CPT), and SNOMED CT. Considered as an outcome measurement, it could still be counted in many situations as a subjective measurement. There is also a degree of variation involved in the coding process. This will be discussed in Section 3.4. Much of the subjectivity is involved in most assessments by healthcare providers and PROs.

Objective measurements are a result of laboratory or physiological monitoring output, and they do not depend on individual interpretation. A structured and direct assessment based on standard definitions and guidelines can be considered as an objective measurement in most situations.

Variation in measurements should be described in the evaluation protocol as it can significantly affect the results and their interpretation.

3.3 Data Collection for Evaluation Studies

Data are a central component of any evaluation study. However, data only become information after appropriate gathering, analysis, and interpretation. Data collection is a crucial step in the whole process. Data collection may be a time- and resource-consuming process if performed manually. The main advantage of data that are already collected is that they will save cost and time. However, it is at the price of potential flaws in terms of quality. It is already predefined how data were recorded, measured, and collected.

Data sources could be divided into two groups:

Primary data: Collected exclusively for this evaluation. The majority of studies for hypothesis testing require the collection of new data since no complete data set exists. The examples would be a prospective collection of observation data or special registers that systematically collect data for the purpose of this particular study.

Secondary data: Data collected or stored for other purposes than the evaluation study and used *secondarily* to answer the study question. Electronic medical records (EMRs) data are an example of this source, since their primary goal is to support patient care.

However, EMRs offer a whole range of unprecedented opportunities to electronically retrieve, collect, and analyze patient information. Other data collection strategies include manual chart review, paper and electronic surveys of patients or providers, phone and in-person interviews, and focus group narratives, as well as direct observation.

Not all data are available in the EMRs or in the revenue cycle system. Fidelity and clinical relevance are different in administrative claims and other high-level summary databases and registers. Based on the evaluation study, the purpose and rationale for data collection should be described in the evaluation protocol (and later in the report). Table 3.1 includes key differentiators in data availability between the EMRs and the revenue cycle system.

Table 3.1 shows that the most valuable data from the perspective of patients and clinicians are in the EMRs.

3.4 Data Quality

The next big question is data quality. Based on the method of data collection, it could be random error or systematic discrepancy. The basic method for data quality control is a random check against the source. Another quick method is statistical control for unusual patterns in data sets.

Usually, there are three different problems with data quality:

1. Missing data: It could be due to the poor quality of the source data (garbage in–garbage out) or insufficient method in data acquisition or handling/manipulation/ merging. Based on the volume of missed data, missed data should be recollected or acknowledged in the limitation section of the resulting manuscript/report.
2. Data availability, consistency, and quality over time: This is a problem with longitudinal studies. Careful planning and appropriate data definitions and dictionaries should be used. In some situations, the difference could be significant to invalidate a measurement.
3. Validity of key data definitions: Clinical definitions used in a study should be trusted and widely accepted. Study staff should be trained to use them consistently.

Table 3.1   Data Availability in the EMR and Administrative Systems (Revenue Cycle System)

Data	EMR	Revenue Cycle System
Demographic information	Yes	Yes
Insurance	Yes	Yes
Allergies	Yes	No
Narrative clinical assessment (clinical notes)	Yes	No
Nurses clinical assessment (nursing flow sheet)	Yes	No
Problem list, hospitalization summary	Yes	No
Diagnoses	Yes	Coded
Surgery, procedures	Narrative and results	Coded
Laboratory	Clinical finding	Coded
Radiology and other diagnostic procedures	Clinical finding	Coded
Orders	Yes, if CPOE implemented	For coding purposes
Medication ordered	Yes	No
Medication list, home medications, medications administered	Yes	No
Medications dispensed	Yes	Yes
Adverse events	Yes	Yes
Physiological data (bedside monitoring)	Yes	No

Special attention should be given if administrative/diagnoses codes are used instead of clinical definition. It is a well-documented problem that coded diagnoses and clinical assessment could have a poor agreement. For example, a study was done on common intensive care unit (ICU) diagnoses. Over a hundred medical records were sent to two senior physicians from independent ICUs, who recoded the diagnoses using the ICD after being trained according to guidelines. These codes were then compared with the original codes, which had been selected by the physician treating the patient. The primary diagnosis was matched by both external coders in 34% of cases, and only 18% of the codes were selected by all three coders.[3]

This could limit the interpretation and validity of studies using coded diagnoses as inclusion criteria or outcome end points.

Suggested Reading

American College of Emergency Physicians. Quality of care and the outcomes management movement. http://www.acep.org/Clinical---Practice-Management/. Quality-of-Care-and-the-Outcomes-Management-Movement/

Grimes DA, Schulz KF. Bias and causal associations in observational research. *Lancet*. 2002;359(9302):248–252. PMID: 11812579.

Whiting P, Rutjes AW, Reitsma JB, Glas AS, Bossuyt PM, Kleijnen J. Sources of variation and bias in studies of diagnostic accuracy: A systematic review. *Ann Intern Med*. 2004;140(3):189–202. PMID: 14757617.

Wilson IB, Cleary PD. Linking clinical variables with health-related quality of life. A conceptual model of patient outcomes. *JAMA*. 1995;273(1):59–65. PMID: 7996652.

Wunsch H, Linde-Zwirble WT, Angus DC. Methods to adjust for bias and confounding in critical care health services research involving observational data. *J Crit Care*. 2006;21(1):1–7. PMID: 16616616.

References

1. Sackett DL. Bias in analytic research. *J Chronic Dis*. 1979;32(1–2):51–63. http://www.ncbi.nlm.nih.gov/pubmed/447779.

2. Guyatt GH, Feeny DH, Patrick DL. Measuring health-related quality of life. *Ann Intern Med.* 1993;118(8):622–629. http://www.ncbi.nlm.nih.gov/pubmed/8452328.

3. Misset B, Nakache D, Vesin A, et al. Reliability of diagnostic coding in intensive care patients. *Crit Care.* 2008;12(4):R95. doi:10.1186/cc6969.

Chapter 4

Analyzing the Results of Evaluation

Statistics has a long history in biomedicine, with interest growing in recent years given the increase in data availability. Desktop software has also evolved recently, and it is now possible to perform many common statistical tests quickly and easily. However, there is an increased danger that statistical methods could be used inappropriately, thereby misleading conclusions. Practical evaluation of healthcare information technology (HIT or health IT) is required, using statistical methods to extract and summarize information from massive amounts of data. It is not uncommon for people to be in denial when it comes to understanding statistical principles, based on their complexity. Many factors contribute to the misunderstanding of statistical principles.

There are many books and resources that explain statistics in an easy to understand manner. The book *Statistics for People Who (Think They) Hate Statistics*, now in its fifth edition, attempts to explain concepts using human-centered language.[1] In this chapter, we describe the basic principles of statistics that would be helpful for HIT evaluation, concentrating on important clinical outcomes.

The essential skills needed to master basic statistical methods include:

- Knowledge of statistical terminology and appropriate usage.
- Skills to determine the appropriate statistical procedures for specified data sets and research design.
- Knowledge and skills to use statistical software with common descriptive and inferential statistical tests.
- Knowledge of the advantages and limitations of specific statistical methods.
- Skills for interpreting data and evaluating the results of statistical conclusions.

We analyze data statistically, and with a simple goal—to find the strongest possible conclusions from the available data. In some situations, it could be done without statistical tests. However, in medicine and areas that involve humans, the biological variability and imprecise differences in measurement methods can be huge. In these situations, making sense of the data and distinguishing signals from noise requires statistical calculations. Statistics also has limitations; if a sample used in a statistical test does not represent the population, then the results of the test cannot be generalizable.

4.1 Fundamental Principles of Statistics

We touched on types of data in Chapter 3. However, data type is an important concept to understand. Type of measurement concept is used across statistics. It is used to decide how to handle data and to choose the appropriate statistical test.

Qualitative (numeric) and quantitative (non-numeric) data predefine how much further they should be handled. There are two large groups of variables: continuous and categorical.

Continuous variables, in theory, can be measured so accurately that there are no gaps between possible values (continuum of values); for example, weight, age, and blood pressure.

Categorical variables can be put into a countable number of categories or different groups. They can be further divided into two main subcategories of scales.

Nominal variables have two or more categories, but do not have order. Examples include gender, or the ABO blood grouping system. *Dichotomous* variables are nominal variables that have only two categories, or levels. Once again, gender can be used as an example.

Ordinal variables have two or more categories, but can also be ordered or ranked. One example is the stages of cancer.

Data Preparation

All data, regardless of the source, require some degree of attention before analysis. The first step is to check data for completeness, homogeneity, accuracy, and inconsistency. The second step is tabulation and classification. Data need to be organized in a format that is understandable by statistical software, then coded based on their type.

Descriptive (Summary) Statistics

Descriptive statistics measures the central tendency and variability of data (dispersion), and consists of methods for organizing and summarizing data (Table 4.1). It is important to remember, however, that it does not explain statistical relationships for causality.

Data Distribution

Normal distribution (or "Gaussian" distribution) is based on the theory that repeated measurements with the same instrument tend to be the same. When all multiple measurements

Table 4.1   Descriptive Statistics Variables

Central Tendency	Definition	Advantages	Disadvantages
Central Tendency			
Mean (average)	Arithmetic mean calculated as the sum of all observations divided by the number of observations	Good for mathematical manipulation	Affected by outliers (extreme variables)
Median	Middle number, with the number of observations equal to above and below	Not sensitive to extreme values	Not very good for mathematical manipulation
Dispersion (Variability)			
Standard deviation (SD)	The value is the average difference of individual values from the sample mean	Good for mathematical manipulation	Affected by non-parametric distribution. Inappropriate for skewed data
Quartile	Data points that divide the data set into four equal groups	Use for understandable description of data variation	Not very good for mathematical manipulation

are plotted, they graph as a bell-shaped symmetrical curve with a single peak in the center (Figure 4.1). When the sample has normal distribution, the mean and the median are the same. Thus, the mean and standard deviation are used for the description of normally distributed data. Parametric

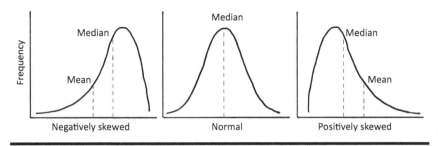

Figure 4.1 Normal and skewed distributions.

statistical methods may also apply for statistical calculations. If the data are skewed, the mean and median are different. The median and interquartile range (IQR) should be used for data description and non-parametric (distribution free) statistical methods.

Probability theory is complex; therefore, additional resources in this chapter link to an online course. However, knowing when and how to utilize the knowledge about distribution is important in order to choose the appropriate statistical test.

Outliers are measurements that have extreme values when compared to the main set of measurements. It is important to check the data for outliers by plotting. Outliers should be handled with a statistical approach (mostly by using a non-parametric test) and cannot be simply deleted because they are higher or lower than expected.

Range and percentiles. Range is the difference between the lowest and highest values in a data set. It is affected by outliers. Percentile is the percentage of observations that is valued between a given percentile. The 95th percentile makes borders for 95% of observations.

Standard deviation (SD) is a measure of the dispersion of a set of data from its mean. The more variability, the higher the deviation. SD is used to illustrate variability in data. It is appropriate to calculate SD on normally distributed data. The Z-score is a number that indicates how many SD data points are from the mean. A Z-score of 2 correlates to an SD of 1.96.

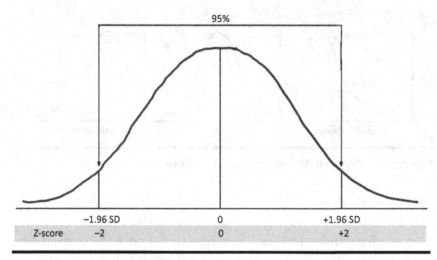

Figure 4.2   Z-scores and SD on the normally distributed data.

In a normally distributed data set, approximately 95% of the data should have a Z-score between –2 and +2. Figure 4.2 shows the relationship between the SD and Z-score. Calculating the Z-score requires knowledge of the mean population and the SD that could be extrapolated from a normally distributed sample.

Interquartile range is often used to describe dispersion in a non-parametric distribution. This difference between the 25th and 75th percentiles includes 50% of observations. A box-and-whisker plot is used as a visualization tool for data description (Figure 4.3).

Confidence Intervals

A confidence interval (CI) is another parameter to describe variability for means and proportions. A 95% CI means that there is 95% confidence that the true population mean lies between those values. It has more practical and clinical implications. Decision making is based not on significance of difference, but on the size of the effect. This gives us an idea from CI limits how clinically important assessing is. Interpretations

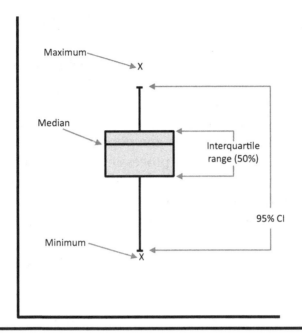

Figure 4.3   Box-and-whisker plot illustrating median, IQR, 95% CI, minimum and maximum values.

also include how wide a CI is. A narrow CI indicates a precise estimate.

p-Value

A p-value helps determine the statistical significance of results and could be any number between 0 and 1. A p-value of ≤ 0.05 (typical level) indicates strong evidence against the null hypothesis. This allows the rejection of the null hypothesis, and supports an alternative hypothesis. The p-value is calculated with statistical software when statistical tests for testing hypotheses are applied. The most-used level of $p < 0.05$ is considered as statistically significant, and $p < 0.001$ as highly statistically significant (as it has a less than one in a thousand chance of being wrong).

4.2 Statistical Tests: Choosing the Right Test

As we search the literature, we can find many different statistical tests that may be confusing. Many of them are not pertinent to biomedicine, or they are complex and require special expertise. However, over the past several decades, as personal computers have become popular, such progress has been made in desktop word processing software that typists can be replaced in many situations. Modern statistical desktop software has become easy enough to use and can therefore carry out the majority of routine statistical tests for health IT evaluation.

The usual process for statistical testing includes several steps:

1. Define outcome variables and null/alternative hypothesis in hypothesis testing study
2. Choose appropriate tests for statistical analysis
3. Collect and prepare data
4. Apply statistical test
5. Interpret statistical significance and results

In the following, we will outline No. 2. Different sources will have slightly different classifications and algorithms for choosing the appropriate statistical tests. They are all correct, but have different ways of approaching the problem based on book goals (clinical epidemiology, statistics, other). As a result, readers would see different charts and tables.

From the perspective of health IT testing, we can break all methods into two large groups: hypothesis tests and analytical tests.

Hypothesis Testing

Experiments with the evaluation project should usually start with research hypotheses. This is a statement of a problem that could be tested with empirical investigation. At the beginning, any null and alternative hypotheses should be stated. A null hypothesis states that there are no differences between two groups (intervention). An alternative hypothesis is opposite to a null hypothesis. There are differences between the two groups (intervention). The goal of the experiment is to find statistical evidence to reject the null hypothesis and support the alternative.

A well-formulated hypothesis should be important, focused, and feasible.

As a result of the statistical test, we should obtain the p-value. If it is statistically significant, then we can reject the null hypothesis and the assumption that there are differences between the groups. The CI can be used in hypothesis testing as a quantifying effect of interest, enabling clinical implication of the results. If the CI does not contain the null hypothesis value, the results are statistically significant.[2]

Non-Parametric Tests

There are two groups of statistical tests for hypothesis testing: parametric and non-parametric. Parametric tests should be used on samples that are normally distributed. If a sample is skewed (it is also helpful if the sample size is small), non-parametric tests (rank-methods) should be used. Non-parametric tests usually rank data and make no assumption about distribution, thus resulting in a less powerful test and a decrease in the tested effect.

One- and Two-Tailed Tests

Some tests have one- and two-tailed versions. Choose one or the other based on the knowledge of what direction the studied effect will change. If there is no absolute knowledge of where intervention (e.g., decrease complication of disease) will lead, then two-tailed tests should be used.

Paired and Independent Tests

Paired or matched samples consist of an observation where one data set is directly related to a specific observation in the other data set. The simplest example is the blood sugar level from the same person before and after treatment. In that situation, paired tests should be used. If samples, independent regular tests should be applied: for example, a comparison of blood sugar levels of all patients in the intensive care unit (ICU), measured in January, followed by measurement again in February when new electronic monitoring tools were implemented, which required independent (not paired) testing.

Number of Comparisons Groups

Another dimension that should be considered for testing is choosing the number of comparison groups: (1) within group, (2) two groups, (3) more than two groups.

The choice of statistical test depends on the number of parameters. However, in general, the following items need to be considered:

■ Number of dependent variables
■ Number of independent variables
■ Dependency: independent or paired data
■ Distribution normality: parametric or non-parametric
■ Type of variables: numerical or categorical

There are no universal or comprehensive algorithms for choosing the appropriate statistical test; however, Table 4.2 summarizes tests for one dependent variable.[3]

Table 4.2 Appropriate Statistical Methods for Hypothesis Testing with One Dependent Variable

Groups	Dependency	Normality	Numerical Data	Categorical Data
One group		Parametric	One-sample *t*-test	Z-test for proportions
		Non-parametric	Wilcoxon signed rank test	Sign test
Two groups	Independent	Parametric	Unpaired *t*-test	Chi-squared test
		Non-parametric	Mann–Whitney U-test (Wilcoxon rank-sum test)	Fisher's exact test
	Paired	Parametric	Paired Student's *t*-test	McNemar's test
		Non-parametric	Wilcoxon signed rank test	
Three+ groups	Independent	Parametric	One way ANOVA	Chi-squared test
		Non-parametric	Kruskal–Wallis test	
	Paired	Parametric	Repeated measures ANOVA	
		Non-parametric	Friedman's test	

Analytics Methods

Identifying Relationship: Correlation

Purpose: Correlation is used to measure the degree of association between two variables.

Methods: Pearson's correlation coefficient calculated for normally distributed data. Non-parametric equivalent is Spearman's correlation.

Interpretation: Test reports *r* (correlation coefficient). *R* ranges from 1 to 1. Zero means that there is no linear correlation between variables; 1 is a perfect positive correlation; 1 is a perfect negative correlation.

Limitations: Correlation cannot be calculated if there is more than one observation from one individual, with outliers presented, the relationship is not linear or data compromise subgroups.

Regression

For many non-statisticians, the terms *correlation* and *regression* are synonymous, and refer vaguely to a mental image of a scatter graph with dots sprinkled messily along a diagonal line sprouting from the intercept of the axes. The term *regression* refers to a mathematical equation that allows one variable (the target variable) to be predicted from another (the independent variable). Regression, then, implies a direction of influence, although it does not prove causality.[4]

Purpose: To identify and quantify the relationship between predictor (independent) variables and outcome (dependent) variables. Predictor variables can also be called risk factors: exposure, intervention, or treatment and outcome variables as outcome events (disease). As a result, regression allows us to build a prediction model.

Linear regression is a technique where only one continuous predictor variable is considered.

Interpretation: Usual output is the *p*-value that is interpreted as evidence against a null hypothesis. There are also 95% CI that could be reported. Correlation coefficient *r* could be reported to estimate the strength of association between the outcome and risk factors.

Multiple regression is a model used to examine the dependency of numerical outcome events on more than one risk factor. Including multiple risk factors in the analysis allows control of confounding factors, and eliminates their impact on exam relationships between study interventions and outcomes.

Logistics regression is a regression technique used to analyze binary outcome variables. The results of logistic regression are presented as odds, rather than as outcome probability.

Limitations and assumptions: All regression methods require independent observations. In addition, linear and multiple regression requires normally distributed data and linearity.

Using logistics methods requires a good understanding of the studied problem as a domain expert or working with a domain expert. Regression methods are important in health IT studies since informatics interventions are rarely applied in isolation. Multiple confounders should be considered and used for analysis. Good free articles available explain regression methods.[5,6]

Longitudinal Studies: Repeated Measures

Longitudinal study involves several observations of the same subjects over a period of time. Data in such studies are collected at the outset of the study, and may then be repeatedly gathered throughout the length of the study.

The analysis of variance (ANOVA) can be used in cases where there are more than two groups that need to be compared. ANOVA compares one or more mean scores with each other to test for the difference in mean scores. Repeated measures ANOVA is a statistical technique that compares means across one or more variables that are based on repeated observations.

Time-to-Event: Survival Analysis

There are often needs to explore how one subject of a study reaches the end point of interest. It could be the result of treatment or death. There are two major characteristics of such studies: length of time to reach the end point, and cen-soring—individuals who left the study for other than the end point reason. Methods such as logistics regression will mislead results because of unique study characteristics. Statistical tech-niques as survival methods should be used in these situations. Two common models are used for survival analysis with binary predictor—Kaplan–Meier curve—and in the case of continuous predictor, Cox proportional hazard model. The log-rank test is often used as a non-parametric test to compare two groups.

Diagnostic Accuracy Studies

Diagnostic accuracy studies are important tools for health IT evaluation. When you develop a new tool for a detection event (alert), you need to compare it with the established best measurement—"the gold standard." This type of study is widely used in laboratory medicine. Sensitivity and specificity are basic measures of diagnostic test performance that should be present together. They describe how well a test can detect if a diagnostic condition is present or absent.

■ Sensitivity is how often the test is positive when the condi-tion of interest is present. Sensitivity = 100% TP/(TP + FN).
■ Specificity is how often the test is negative when the con-dition of interest is absent. Specificity = 100% TN/(FP + TN).

Other important metrics of testing are positive and negative predictive values (PPV, NPV), likelihood ratios (LRs), and the area under the receiver operating characteristic (ROC) curve (area under the curve [AUC]).

■ PPV defines the probability of having the disease of interest in a subject with a positive result: PPV = (TP/TP + FP).
■ NPV defines the probability of not having the disease in a subject with a negative test result: NPV = (TN/TN + FN).

Predictive values are largely dependent on disease prevalence in the examined population.

Positive and negative LR is a measure of diagnostic accuracy. LR interpretation is how many times more likely a particular test results in subjects with the disease than in those without the disease.

■ Positive LR ratio is (LR+ = sensitivity/(1–specificity)).
■ Negative LR ratio is (LR– = (1–sensitivity)/specificity).

The standard way of summarizing the results of diagnostic performance studies is the 2-by-2 contingency table. The relationships between the diagnostic test (alert) and the occurrence of disease or event are shown in Figure 4.4.

ROC curves show the ability of the diagnostic test to correctly classify subjects as different levels of threshold. The ROC curve is a plot of the sensitivity and specificity values for every individual point. The shape of an ROC curve and the

		Disease or event (reference standard)	
		Present	Absent
Test or alert (new test)	Positive	True positive	False positive
	Negative	False negative	True negative

Figure 4.4 Relationship between diagnostic test or alert and the occurrence of disease or event.

calculated AUC estimate the discriminative power of a test. The closer the curve is located to the upper left corner and the larger the AUC, the better the test for discriminating between diseased and non-diseased. A perfect diagnostic test has an AUC of 1.0. AUC 0.5 is an equal flip of the coin.

The Food and Drug Administration (FDA) has an excellent document called "Statistical Guidance on Reporting Results from Studies Evaluating Diagnostic Tests" that also describes the terminology and processes for estimation of agreement with a non-reference standard (http://www.fda.gov/MedicalDevices/DeviceRegulationandGuidance/GuidanceDocuments/ucm071148.htm).

Assessing Agreements

Kappa is used to assess reproducibility or inter-rater reliability. One example would be the agreement between two observers on the same measurements.[7] Kappa used on categorical variables and values greater than 0.75 is considered as excellent agreement. A more advanced statistical method is intraclass correlation coefficient (ICC), which is applicable for assessing inter-rater reliability, with two or more raters.

The *Bland–Altman plot* is a method of comparing new measurement techniques with an established one to see whether they agree sufficiently for the new to replace the old. This is a graphical method where the differences between the two continuous variables are plotted against their averages.[8]

Outcome Measurements

The statistical outcome measurement selection involves a selection of metrics, which is important to show improvement in patient outcomes. The association between specific intervention and clinical outcome is described by other metrics, rather than by statistical inference.[9] The process and definition linked to evidence-based medicine (EBM) have identified four major clinical processes: harm, diagnosis, therapy, and prognosis.

When you develop a meaningful informatics tool, the target of such a tool is improving upon one of those processes. To be able to show the impact on patient-centered outcomes, the health IT tool should show improvement in one of those statistics.

1. *Harm*: We must often make judgments as to whether environmental agents or medical interventions could be harmful. A study with design as cohort studies, case controls, or a randomized controlled trial (RCT) could answer this question.

   For example, in health IT, researchers introduce software that is designed to notify office workers to take breaks, with the goal of reducing computer vision syndrome (CVS).[10] To be able to show the clinical usefulness of this application, a prospective RCT trial would be the ideal intervention, but case control could be acceptable as well. However, to show the ability of this application to prevent CVS, results should show a decrease in relative risk—relative risk reduction or a change in the odds ratio within the case-control study.

   In randomized trials and cohort studies, relative risk is calculated as (RR) = EER/CER (Table 4.3). It is the risk (or incidence) of the adverse event in the exposed (or treated) patients, relative to that in the unexposed (or untreated) patients.

   In case-control studies, because it is not proof, causality odds ratio should be calculated: (OR) = (a*d)/(b*c).

   Statistical significance is calculated using 95% CI. If RR or OR has a crossed value of 1, it means that there is no effect.

2. *Diagnosis and screening*: We have previously discussed diagnostic performance studies. They are the study of

Table 4.3 Calculating Effects of Experimental Intervention Using 2-by-2 Table

	Outcome/Adverse Event		
	Yes/Case/ Present	No/Absent/ Control	
Experimental group/ exposure: Yes	a	b	Experimental event rate (EER) = risk of outcome event in experimental group = a/(a + b)
Control group/ exposure: No	c	d	Control event rate (CER) = risk of outcome event in control group = c/(c + d)

choice for the comparison of new alert/detection/prediction algorithms with the current "gold standard."

3. *Treatment/therapy*: This type of question arose from "interventional" technology. If technology is supposed to treat a patient's condition, then it should be evaluated in clinical trials. Design is varied and depends on many factors; however, some common statistics should be calculated to show the benefits of treatment (intervention). The 2-by-2 table used for the calculation of such statistics is show in Table 4.3.

To quantify benefits, some numbers should be calculated:

Relative risk reduction (RRR): Measurement of how treatment reduces risk in comparison with patients not receiving the treatment of interest: (RRR) = (CER EER)/CER.

Absolute risk reduction (ARR): The difference in the rates of adverse events between experimental and control populations: (ARR) = CER EER.

Number needed to treat (NNT): The number of patients who must be treated with experimental intervention in order to prevent one adverse outcome: (NNT) = 1/ARR = 1/(CER EER).

ARR is the most clinically relevant measure and NNT is the most useful measurement of benefits.

4. *Prognosis*: Prognosis is the prediction of the disease and its outcome. Survival analysis and time-to-event types of analysis are appropriate for assessment as we have previously discussed. Outside of the ultimate negative outcomes such as death, recurrence, and remission, health-related quality of life could be calculated. Clinical prediction rules ideally should be compared by time-to-event analysis.

Other Statistical Considerations

Statistics is a diverse field with many nuances. Here, we introduce three items that are important to keep in mind.

Multiple Comparisons

Often, when we have data, we would like to do many comparisons to find statistically significant relationships. The Type I error increases dramatically, which leads to spurious conclusions. Analysis should be included only in a limited number of tests to answer the study hypothesis. This is becoming more obvious with data-mining exercises to find something significant. The *p*-value must be adjusted by using Bonferroni correction, or multivariate methods such as ANOVA should be used.

Subgroup Analysis

Another type of analysis that could lead to the wrong conclusions if not done correctly is subgroup analysis. Subgroup analyses split data into subgroups and make comparisons between them; for example, in order to show that intervention has an effect on females over age 55, but not in other groups. There are three common types of subgroup analysis that could be performed for different reasons:

Confirmatory: Test stated *a priori* hypothesis about subgroup effects.

Descriptive: Describe subgroup for future evaluation and synthesis.

Exploratory: Identify subgroup for future hypotheses evaluation.

When conducting subgroup analyses, it is important to address the heterogeneity of effect.

Sample Size Calculation

An essential part of preparation for any evaluation is sample size calculation—planning how many study subjects must be included to answer a posed question. Without the numeric rationale for the study size, lack of a statistically significant difference could give a false perception of lack of harm, or a false conclusion about the comparison of two interventions. Sample size calculation should not be done by guessing. Unjustified large sample sizes are a waste of time and money and pose additional risk to study subjects. Different techniques are applied for the processing of sample size calculation; however, they require content expertise in their studied domain.[11]

Commonly Used Statistical Tools

Progress with desktop operation systems has brought about a number of statistical software packages that have become available to the masses.

SAS (https://www.sas.com) is considered the "gold standard" in statistical calculation, and features a desktop version. However,

SAS could be recommended more for users whose daily duties include statistical analysis. It is an expensive enterprise solution.

JMP (http://www.jmp.com) is desktop software developed by SAS. It is a powerful tool for data retrieval, preparation, and analytical work. It can perform most statistical analyses; however, there are longer learning curves, as it is not very intuitive for the novice user.

SPSS (http://www-01.ibm.com/software/analytics/spss/) is a widely used statistical tool in biomedicine. It performs almost all analysis, which could be required for the average power user.

MedCalc (https://www.medcalc.org/) can be seen as the extraction of the most important analytics techniques in biomedicine. It is easy to use and features a robust help system. It is recommended for users who do analysis as part of an evaluation or research process.

GraphPad Prism (http://www.graphpad.com/scientific-software/prism/) and InStat (http://www.graphpad.com/scientific-software/instat/) are two software products from one company. GraphPad has most of the commonly used statistical tests embedded within it. InStat is more of a user-guidance dialogue system.

Tableau (http://www.tableau.com/) is a rapid analytics and visualization tool that has some basic statistical functions. The power of this software is in its quick, yet flexible ability to visualize data.

After commercial statistical software, free software programs are also available (SciDAVis, QtiPlot, LabPlot); however, they have limited usability. R language is widely used for data analysis, but requires programming skills.

Suggested Reading

Four articles "Basic statistics for clinicians" in *Canadian Medical Association Journal*. PMIDs: 7804919, 7820798, 7828099, 7859197.

Online statistical calculators. http://graphpad.com/quickcalcs/ GraphPad.

Online Statistics Education: An Interactive Multimedia Course of Study. http://onlinestatbook.com/.

Open introductory course to biostatistics. Lectures slides in PDF and audio. http://ocw.jhsph.edu/index.cfm/go/viewCourse/course/ IntroBiostats/coursePage/index/.

Statistics: How to. Great education materials including video. http:// www.statisticshowto.com/.

Statistical reference from StatsDirect software. http://www.statsdi-rect.com/help/.

Statistics review. Series of 14 articles published in *Critical Care* journal. Links to full text: http://www.ccforum.com/series/ CC_Medical.

Teaching materials on probability. Methods of sampling, basic concepts of probability, and applications of probability theory. http://sphweb.bumc.bu.edu/otlt/MPH-Modules/BS/BS704_ Probability/index.html.

References

1. Salkind NJ. *Statistics for People Who (Think They) Hate Statistics*. Los Angeles, CA: SAGE, 2014.
2. Gardner MJ, Altman DG. Confidence intervals rather than P values: Estimation rather than hypothesis testing. *Br Med J (Clin Res Ed)*. 1986;292(6522):746–750. http://www.ncbi.nlm.nih.gov/ pubmed/3082422.
3. Nayak BK, Hazra A. How to choose the right statistical test? *Indian J Ophthalmol*. 59(2):85–86.
4. Greenhalgh T. How to read a paper. Statistics for the non-statistician. II: "Significant" relations and their pitfalls. *BMJ*. 1997;315(7105):422–425. http://www.pubmedcentral.nih.gov/arti-clerender.fcgi?artid=2127270&#x0026;tool=pmcentrez&#x0026;rendertype=abstract. Accessed September 15, 2011.
5. Bewick V, Cheek L, Ball J. Statistics review 14: Logistic regression. *Crit Care*. 2005;9(1):112–118.
6. Bewick V, Cheek L, Ball J. Statistics review 7: Correlation and regression. *Crit Care*. 2003;7(6):451–459.

7. Viera AJ, Garrett JM. Understanding interobserver agreement: The kappa statistic. *Fam Med.* 2005;37(5):360–363. http://www. ncbi.nlm.nih.gov/pubmed/15883903.

8. Bland JM, Altman DG. Statistical methods for assessing agreement between two methods of clinical measurement. *Lancet.* 1986;1(8476):307–310. http://www.ncbi.nlm.nih.gov/ pubmed/2868172.

9. Schechtman E. Odds ratio, relative risk, absolute risk reduction, and the number needed to treat—which of these should we use? *Value Health.* 5(5):431–436.

10. Julius N, Mustapha EE. Take-A-Break Notification: An ergo-nomic application. In: *Proceedings of the 6th International Conference on Information Technology and Multimedia.* Vol. IEEE; 2014:390–395.

11. Scales DC, Rubenfeld GD. Estimating sample size in critical care clinical trials. *J Crit Care.* 2005;20(1):6–11. http://www.ncbi. nlm.nih.gov/pubmed/16015511.

Chapter 5

Proposing and Communicating the Results of Evaluation Studies

The final product of any healthcare information technology (HIT or health IT) evaluation project is a report in the broad sense of the word. A well-done evaluation report is a powerful instrument. It can affect commitment to funding, stakeholders' engagement, future commercialization, and, eventually, real-world applicability to influencing practice and health outcomes. Depending on their main goals, evaluation reports could have different focuses and target audiences. Regardless of this, ideal reports have key elements that allow their transformation or conversion into other types if necessary. Essential starting points should be addressed in the following documents before a project is actually started:

1. Project proposal
2. Detailed protocol

3. Standard operating procedures (SOP)
4. Study journal/log

Understanding the report preparation process and its goals will help to polish the study protocol and minimize the burden on later stages of the project.

As you start to prepare a report, a clear message is a key factor for success. Message must be consistent regardless of method and media for results dissemination. The style can vary based on the target audience, but it should always be high in quality and follow basic structural rules.

5.1 Target Audience

A final evaluation report has a readership that extends beyond stakeholders—people with vested interests. Additional readers who may be interested in the results of the evaluation include policy-makers, the scientific community, and a general audience/society. The matrix in Table 5.1 indicates types of reports and their intended audiences.

5.2 Methods of Dissemination

As outlined in Table 5.1, there are different modalities for "printed" communication. All of them are supposed to deliver the same message but at different lengths and with different focuses and levels of details.

Abstract: This is a scientific summary that outlines major information concerning study goals, methods, and results.

Scientific peer-reviewed article: This detailed publication about a study has standard elements. It undergoes peer review and the scientific community considers it a final study "product."

Table 5.1 Types of Study Reports and Their Target Audiences

	Patients and Family	Clinicians	IT and Security	Administrators/ Purchasers	Scientific Community	Policy-makers	General Audience/ Society
Abstract		X			X		
Scientific peer-reviewed article		X			X		
Newsletter article	X			X		X	X
Evaluation report			X	X		X	
Poster		X			X		
Website publication	X			X			X
Guideline/ standard		X	X			X	

Newsletter article: A journalist usually writes one based on the available information. The journalist prepares it in such a way that a lay audience can understand it.

Evaluation report: This is the final "product" of an administratively ordered evaluation. It may have robust details.

Poster: This is usually a scientifically based visual report for presentation at different events. The granularity of its details lies between that of a full article and that of an abstract with additional visual components.

Website publication: This broad media platform is usually not restricted in size (unlike a newsletter publication). It could target any audience. Outside of official scientific journals, publications of this type are mostly not peer reviewed.

Guideline/standard: Rarely, one evaluation study could form the basis for a guideline. However, it could serve as a company/organization standard.

All of these modalities have different preparation times, granularities, and styles. Not only does producing a robust protocol from the beginning help one to perform a high-quality study, but it also helps in the much quicker development of any publication product.

5.3 Universal, Scientifically Based Outline for the Dissemination of Evaluation Study Results

Structuring a publication is the most difficult part of writing whether the document in question is a report, a scientific paper, or a fiction novel. If the structure is logical and correct, everything else follows. If, however, the structure is weak or illogical, no amount of clever, complex language can compensate for that. Structure is necessary so that readers do not get lost.[1]

Scientific papers in medical journals typically follow the IMRAD structure: Introduction, Methods, Results, *and*

Discussion. Using this template for the preparation of a publication allows the production of a high-quality data-driven publication regardless of its target audience. Structured language can be adapted for a specific audience and type of report much more easily than writing without any structure. Next, we explain every aspect of that structure.

Title: This should be the focus of the evaluation question, and it should be representative. Avoid misleading and PR-style titles.

Introduction: This part should be very clear without unnecessary, irrelevant, or very high-level statistical details. The following elements should always be included in at least one phrase each. Avoid including anything that does not fit among these four elements.

- Background of the study. This entails information about the overall topic of evaluation. Limit it to important details and avoid trivialities and clichés.
- Previous studies in the area. It is important to include relevant information, starting from general education to specific information and in chronological order. If no previous research exists in the area, explain why. Always cite landmark articles in the field. Limit citations to a maximum of 10. This is not a literature review.
- Problems in a field and specific topic. Describe why you performed this evaluation. Indicate what the knowledge gap is and what was not done or was done wrong in the existing research (e.g., a different setting, a weak design, or insufficient measurements). This should not include critiques or misleading statements, only facts.
- How your evaluation study addressed the problem. Explain how you improved on past studies.

The introduction should end with a declaration of specific aims and one or two study overview sentences.

Methods: The methods section is logically linked to the results. Overall, in this section, you must describe how you measured your results.

- Design. What type of study was performed? Define the study based on the clinical epidemiology classification: cross-sectional (descriptive) study, case-control study, cohort study, trial (randomized, before-and-after, non-randomized), or diagnostic performance study. Indicate whether the study was prospective or retrospective.
- Subjects. Whom or what did you study? Specify where you held the study and how you chose the subjects. List the inclusion and exclusion criteria as well as the study time line. Be very specific about how you defined the groups: cases, controls, or randomization. If a study involved human subjects (not only patients but also clinicians and employees), indicate whether it received approval or a waiver from the Institutional Review Board (IRB). Quality studies could receive other forms of approval. Consult your IRB or legal department.
- Measurement. What was measured? Present the measurements in logical order, starting from predictor variables to outcome variables (which may be primary or secondary). Describe how the variables were measured. If the study is interventional, describe the study procedures, including the quality of the measurements. Describe how the data were collected and stored.
- Analysis. How was the data analyzed? Describe how and why you analyzed the data.
  - Effect size. Discuss how the sample size and effect size were estimated.
  - Who was analyzed? Indicate whether or not an intention-to-treat analysis was adopted for clinical trials.
  - Variable transformation and adjustment. What approach was taken to analyze data?

- Intention-to-treat, non-parametric, matching, stratification.
- Power. Define the power of the study and its level of significance. Describe how the statistical significance was calculated.
- Software. Indicate what software was used for analysis.

Results: The results should be reported around the main findings of the evaluation, not around the significant *p*-values. Describe the findings solely. Leave the interpretation of the results and their meaning for the discussion section.

For descriptive results, report based on the type of data. For dichotomous and categorical variables, provide the count and percentage. It may also include the risk ratio, rate, incidence, prevalence, or odds. For continuous variables, include the central tendency and the variance. For normally distributed data, report the mean and SD. For skewed data and non-parametric tests, report the median and the interquartile range (IQR). Use the appropriate units and limit the decimal digits for the appropriate level of precision.

For analytic results, compare two or more variables using the appropriate statistical method. Indicate the precision of an estimate by using the confidence interval. In addition, indicate the level of significance using the *p*-value.

Include tables and figures as needed. The general rule is to include tables or figures for better presentation, emphasis, and readability. Do not repeat the same data in tables and figures and text.

Discussion: This is an important but difficult part to write. It requires deep understanding of the problem and domain expertise. The structure of the discussion must include the following:

■ Principal findings. What did you find? In the initial paragraph of the discussion, provide one or two statements about the implications of the findings. That will provide a framework for the rest of the discussion. Explain the key findings of the evaluation and describe other important findings.

■ Meaning of the study. What do you think the results mean, and how strongly do you believe them? This is where you should interpret the results and indicate how convincing they are. If you have found an association between a predictor and an outcome, explain the possible mechanism for that association (chance, bias, effect-cause, effect-effect, or cause-effect).

■ Comparison with prior studies. How do your results compare to prior knowledge? Synthesize the results of prior studies, but do not undertake a literature review. Pick the most important and relevant studies. Explain why your findings are different or similar to those of other studies. What are their strengths and weaknesses in relation to those of other studies? Do not overcritique other studies' limitations.

■ Strengths and weaknesses of the study. What are the limitations? Every study has problems, and authors must identify those that may affect the validity or meaning of the study. Explain them; do not just list them. Focus on the methodological issues. What is potentially avoidable, what is not, and how does this affect the current study?

■ Unanswered questions and future research. What are the findings' implications for stakeholders and broader groups, and what should be done next?

The discussion should be based on the scope of the data and on previous publications. Keep speculation to a minimum, but explain how findings and data can provide the basis for future research. Include this within the flow of the discussion, not in one place at the end.

Conclusion: "Take-home message." This is a conclusive statement of findings based on actual results, not on the expected results. It should be a brief statement of implication followed by future plans.

5.4 Reporting Standards and Guidelines

Back in 1993, a group of experts met with the aim of developing a new scale to assess the quality of randomized controlled trial (RCT) reports. That resulted in the development of the Consolidated Standards of Reporting Trials (CONSORT) statement, which was published in 1996.[2] This guideline was organized around a checklist and was revised twice (Table 5.2).

In 2010, CONSORT reporting criteria were revised for their relevance to eHealth RCT. STARE-HI (Statement on the Reporting of Evaluation Studies in Health Informatics) was adopted. The statement was developed and published.[3] In reality, it did not represent a dramatic change from the usual RCT reporting. That is, it confirmed the role of clinical epidemiology research principals in the evaluation of health IT.

The success of CONSORT-type guides led to the establishment of Enhancing the QUAlity and Transparency Of health Research (EQUATOR) network (http://www.equator-network. org/). This is an international initiative that seeks to improve the reliability and value of published health research literature by promoting transparent and accurate reporting and wider use of robust reporting guidelines. This is a starting point and a "one stop shop" free resource.

When you prepare a scientific publication, it is best practice to follow those guidelines. Many journals require the submission of a checklist with indications of the pages on which all elements are addressed.

For a HIT evaluation, the following guidelines would be helpful:

■ The Consolidated Health Economic Evaluation Reporting Standards (CHEERS) statement.[5]

Table 5.2 CONSORT-Selected Criteria Adapted for eHealth RCTs

No.	Element	Explanation
Title and Abstract		
1a		Identification as a randomized trial in the title
1b		Structured summary of trial design, methods, results, and conclusions (for specific guidance see CONSORT for abstracts)
	Introduction	
2a	Background and objectives	Scientific background and explanation of rationale
2b		Specific objectives or hypotheses
Methods		
3a	Trial design	Description of trial design (e.g., parallel, factorial) including allocation ratio
3b		Important changes to methods after trial commencement (such as eligibility criteria), with reasons
4a	Participants	Eligibility criteria for participants
4b		Settings and locations where the data were collected
5	Interventions	The interventions for each group with sufficient details to allow replication, including how and when they were actually administered
6a	Outcomes	Completely defined prespecified primary and secondary outcome measures, including how and when they were assessed
6b		Any changes to trial outcomes after the trial commenced, with reasons

(Continued)

Table 5.2 (Continued)   CONSORT-Selected Criteria Adapted for eHealth RCTs

No.	Element	Explanation
7a	Sample size	How sample size was determined
7b		When applicable, explanation of any interim analyses and stopping guidelines
Randomization		
8a	Sequence generation	Method used to generate the random allocation sequence
8b		Type of randomization; details of any restriction (such as blocking and block size)
9	Allocation concealment mechanism	Mechanism used to implement the random allocation sequence (such as sequentially numbered containers), describing any steps taken to conceal the sequence until interventions were assigned
10	Implementation	Who generated the random allocation sequence, who enrolled participants, and who assigned participants to interventions?
11a	Blinding	If done, who was blinded after assignment to interventions (e.g., participants, care providers, those assessing outcomes) and how?
11b		If relevant, description of the similarity of interventions
12a	Statistical methods	Statistical methods used to compare groups for primary and secondary outcomes
12b		Methods for additional analyses, such as subgroup analyses and adjusted analyses

(Continued)

Table 5.2 (Continued)   CONSORT-Selected Criteria Adapted for eHealth RCTs

No.	Element	Explanation
Results		
13a	Participant flow (a diagram is strongly recommended)	For each group, the numbers of participants who were randomly assigned, received intended treatment, and were analyzed for the primary outcome
13b		For each group, losses and exclusions after randomization, together with reasons
14a	Recruitment	Dates defining the periods of recruitment and follow-up
14b		Why the trial ended or was stopped
15	Baseline data	A table showing baseline demographic and clinical characteristics for each group
16	Numbers analyzed	For each group, number of participants (denominator) included in each analysis and whether the analysis was by original assigned groups
17a	Outcomes and estimation	For each primary and secondary outcome, results for each group and the estimated effect size and its precision (such as 95% confidence interval)
17b		For binary outcomes, presentation of both absolute and relative effect sizes is recommended

(Continued)

Table 5.2 (Continued)   CONSORT-Selected Criteria Adapted for eHealth RCTs

No.	Element	Explanation
18	Ancillary analyses	Results of any other analyses performed, including subgroup analyses and adjusted analyses, distinguishing prespecified from exploratory
19	Harms	All important harms or unintended effects in each group (for specific guidance see CONSORT for harms)
Discussion		
20	Limitations	Trial limitations, addressing sources of potential bias, imprecision, and, if relevant, multiplicity of analyses
21	Generalizability	Generalizability (external validity, applicability) of the trial findings
22	Interpretation	Interpretation consistent with results, balancing benefits and harms, and considering other relevant evidence
Other Information		
23	Registration	Registration number and name of trial registry
24	Protocol	Where the full trial protocol can be accessed, if available
25	Funding	Sources of funding and other support (such as supply of drugs), role of funders

Source: From Baker, T.B. et al., *Patient Educ Couns.*, 81, S77–S86, 2010[4].

- The Strengthening the Reporting of Observational Studies in Epidemiology (STROBE) statement: Guidelines for reporting observational studies.[6]
- Toward complete and accurate reporting of studies of diagnostic accuracy: The STARD Initiative.[7]

5.5 Other Communication Methods

Evaluation Report: This mostly serves as a closed or limited circulation document for stakeholders and the funding body. In principle, this is a deeper version of the scientific manuscript with more details in the methodologies and results sections, including the SOP and full protocol. Also, result inclusion is more extensive. Analytical parts, such as the literature review and interpretation, depend on the scope of the report. However, a good evaluation report should follow all principles of scientific documentation.

Abstract: An abstract is a critical part of a full manuscript or separate publication. Usually, it is limited to between 250 and 300 words. Many people only read the abstracts to get an idea of the full publication. Also, database and search engines index abstracts alone. It is crucial to have a high-quality abstract with sufficient details. An abstract is based on the IMRAD concept but written with word limitations.

Poster: A poster is a visual media communication tool. It is usually presented at a scientific meeting, but it could also be used as a permanent display. In the academic world, a poster is often viewed as a less prestigious type of presentation. However, from the perspective of the dissemination of a health IT evaluation study, a well-prepared poster is a very powerful tool. The obvious advantage is that a much larger audience could view a poster than an oral presentation. People who are interested in a particular work could discuss it with the author of the poster or get in touch later.

A poster should be prepared with some specific details in mind. First, it is not a copy of the abstract or a short version of the full manuscript. A poster is a visual communication tool. It should be designed in such a way as to attract people (encouraging them to stop by) and give them an information overview in a couple of seconds. If they are interested, they can read the details. That is the concept of "visual layers." Second, the writing should be redesigned as bullet points and "easy phrases." This communicates the given idea, and, if more information is needed, the poster author can provide it through speech or a proceedings/abstract book can address the details. Third, it should be legible from a distance. The font should not be small. Figure 5.1 indicates the essential elements of posters.

Diagrams—displaying data: Diagrams are excellent tools for data summarization and present bigger arrays of information in an easy and understandable manner. Not every number should be translated into a diagram. In many situations, a table is a better choice. However, there are some good practice rules. A diagram is preferred for printed media such as articles and is better for multiple variables and showing summaries and central tendencies. Diagrams perform better in visual presentations when there are only a couple of variables and it is useful to show all data (patterns).

When you are considering how to best present data, you should ask three questions:

1. What exactly do I need to show?
2. Which methods are available for such data?
3. Is there a preferred method?

The decision should be based on the type of data, the goal of presentation and the evaluators' judgment, and the style. Figure 5.2 shows the types of diagrams that are preferred for specific data. This is obviously not a comprehensive list; however, it covers major types of classical data analysis.

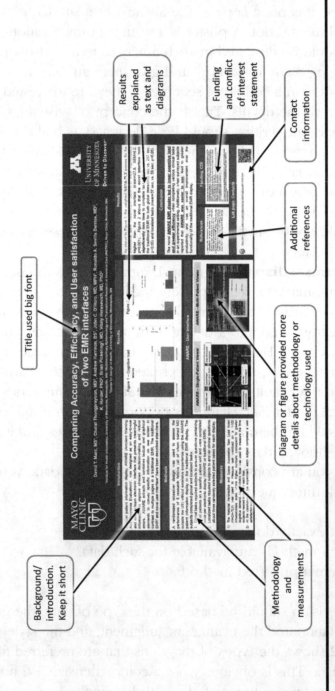

Figure 5.1   Elements of poster (prepared by authors).

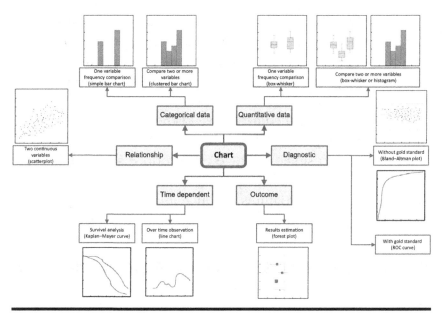

Figure 5.2 How to choose the right/preferred diagram based on specific data.

- Bar charts are preferred to pie charts. Avoid using them.
- Include the total number of subjects, not just percentages.
- Do not use 3-D charts.
- Use shadows of color (gray scale) rather than colors or patterns.
- If color is required, use color-blind safe colors. In the population, 5%–8% of people have color-recognition problems.

Information visualization—infographics: In recent years, a new visualization technique has become incredibly popular—it is called infographics. Infographics are intended to present information quickly and clearly. They constitute a powerful tool for telling data-driven stories. However, the use of this technique should be limited and justifiable. It leans more toward being data-driven art than structured scientific diagrams. Infographics should be used wisely in brief executive reports, white papers, and newsletters and on websites.

There are no rules concerning content, which a specialist designer develops. Figure 5.3 shows an example of infographics. The media and government agencies currently use infographics to support messages and get points across to their audiences.

(https://www.flickr.com/photos/gdsdigital/4016463012/in/ photostream/—by GDS Infographics [CC BY 4.0 license].)

Software: No single package can produce all types of diagrams. Typically, a statistical package should be used for visualization. Statistical programs produce informative diagrams, but they mostly lack attractive designs. Some tools facilitate the

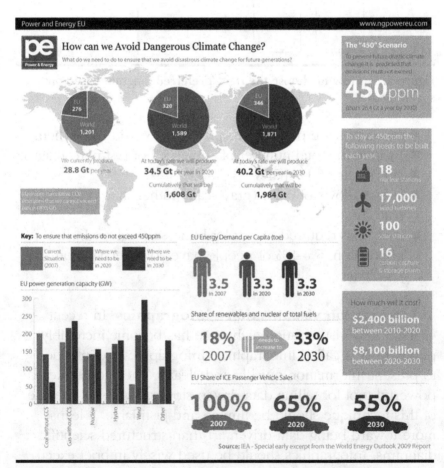

Figure 5.3 An example of infographics (converted to gray scale).

production of high-quality diagrams without extensive skills. Surprisingly, Microsoft PowerPoint can cover most of the diagramming needs for health IT evaluation reports (the majority of this book's illustrations were drawn in MS PowerPoint). More advanced software packages are MS Visio and Edraw Max, but both are only available for MS Windows operating systems. The free open-source multi-platform Pencil (http://pencil.evolus.vn/) is a very robust tool for drawing schemas and diagrams. For color adjustment, picture resizing, and other imaging tasks, there are two easy-to-use Windows applications: XnView (http://www.xnview.com/en/) and FastStone Image Viewer (http://www.faststone.org/). Macintosh users can use XnViewMP.

For infographics, a number of online tools allow one to compile simple visualizations. Start with https://venngage.com, http://piktochart.com, https://infogr.am and http://visme.co.

Oral presentations: One of the key methods of message delivery is oral presentation. It is an effective form of communication and can be recorded, stored, and distributed. Presentation slides can also be archived and saved for future use. A health IT evaluation project may be presented at different stages: project proposal, work in progress update, and final results. A number of excellent books have been published on presentation design and slide preparation. We have listed three of them in the Suggested Reading section of this chapter.

The basic rules for good presentation design include:

1. Simplicity: You are a presenter. The audience should not read from your slides. They are solely for illustration and anchors. Do not read slides as if they were newspapers.
2. Font: The size should be big enough: not less than 24pt in MS PowerPoint.
3. Color: Use no more than three colors. Use them to highlight important points, including text.
4. Background: In most situations, use two solid colors for background: white or dark blue. Using black on white

and yellow/white on dark blue will give a high-contrast and color-blind safe combination.

5. Consistence: Line, fonts, everything.
6. Practice and see No. 1 again.

For different goals and audiences, there are different presentation structures.

1. Project proposal: Use the most influential techniques. Include infographics.
2. Work in progress: Include the fine details of the project and a limited amount of background information.
3. Final report: The actual structure should follow a typical scientific format for presentation:

■ Motivation (Introduction and Background)
■ Problem Statement (Aims)
■ Approach (Methodology)
■ Results (Results)
■ Conclusions (Discussion and Results)

Scalable format: A correctly structured and designed presentation could be scaled for a 5-, 20-, or 60-min speech. Design slide sets with 5-min outlines, then provide more granular details. Following this structure and approach allows easy conversion of presentations for different audiences, such as stakeholders with different focuses or a broader scientific/professional audience.

Suggested Reading

Bossuyt PM, Reitsma JB, Bruns DE, et al. Towards complete and accurate reporting of studies of diagnostic accuracy: The STARD Initiative. *Ann Intern Med*. 2003 Jan 7;138(1):40–44. http://www.ncbi.nlm.nih.gov/entrez/query.fcgi?cmd=Retrieve&db=PubMed&dopt=Citation&list_uids=12513043.

Freeman, JV, Walters SJ, Campbell MJ. *How to Display Data*. Malden, MA: BMJ Books, 2008. ISBN: 978-1405139748.

Guide to choice visualization method. Abela AV, Radich PJ. *Encyclopedia of Slide Layouts*. Great Falls, VA: Soproveitto Press, 2014. ISBN: 978-0996001380.

Overview of abstract writing. Andrade C. How to write a good abstract for a scientific paper or conference presentation. *Indian J Psychiatry*. 2011 Apr;53(2):172–175. PMID: 21772657.

Overview of publication structure. Simera I, Altman DG. Reporting medical research. *Int J Clin Pract*. 2013 Aug;67(8):710–716. PMID: 23656235.

Sechrest L, Backer T, Rogers E, Campbell T, Grady M, editors. *Effective Dissemination of Clinical Health Information*. AHCPR Publication No. 95-0015. Rockville, MD: Public Health Service Agency for Health Care Policy and Research; 1994. Materials of 1994 conference on the topic.

The Journal of the American Medical Association (JAMA) Users' Guides to the Medical Literature: Full list with links. http://med.ubc.ca/files/2012/04/JAMA-Users-Guides-to-the-Medical-Literature.pdf.

Tips and advice for achieving better quality reports. Guyatt GH, Haynes BR. Preparing reports for publication and responding to reviewers' comments. *J Clin Epidemiol*. 2006 Sep;59(9):900–906. PMID: 16895811.

Tips for designing scientific figures for color blind readers. http://www.somersault1824.com/tips-for-designing-scientific-figures-for-color-blind-readers/Books

Wong DM. *The Wall Street Journal Guide to Information Graphics, The Dos and Don'ts of Presenting Data, Facts, and Figures*. New York: W.W. Norton, 2013. ISBN: 9780393347289.

Books on the Presentation Design

Duarte N. *Slide:ology: The Art and Science of Creating Great Presentations*. Sebastopol, CA: O'Reilly Media, 2008. ISBN: 978-0596522346.

Duarte N. *Resonate: Present Visual Stories That Transform Audiences*. Hoboken, NJ: Wiley, 2010. ISBN: 978-0470632017.

References

1. A proposal for more informative abstracts of clinical articles. Ad Hoc Working Group for Critical Appraisal of the Medical Literature. *Ann Intern Med*. 1987;106(4):598–604. http://www.ncbi.nlm.nih.gov/pubmed/3826959.
2. Begg C, Cho M, Eastwood S, et al. Improving the quality of reporting of randomized controlled trials. The CONSORT statement. *JAMA*. 1996;276(8):637–639. http://www.ncbi.nlm.nih.gov/pubmed/8773637.
3. Talmon J, Ammenwerth E, Brender J, de Keizer N, Nykänen P, Rigby M. STARE-HI: Statement on reporting of evaluation studies in health informatics. *Int J Med Inform*. 2009;78(1):1–9.
4. Baker TB, Gustafson DH, Shaw B, et al. Relevance of CONSORT reporting criteria for research on eHealth interventions. *Patient Educ Couns*. 2010;81 Suppl: S77–S86.
5. Husereau D, Drummond M, Petrou S, et al. Consolidated Health Economic Evaluation Reporting Standards (CHEERS) statement. *Eur J Heal Econ*. 2013;14(3):367–372.
6. von Elm E, Altman DG, Egger M, Pocock SJ, Gotzsche PC, Vandenbroucke JP. The Strengthening the Reporting of Observational Studies in Epidemiology (STROBE) statement: Guidelines for reporting observational studies. *Ann Intern Med*. 2007;147(4):344–349.
7. Bossuyt PM, Reitsma JB, Bruns DE, et al. Towards complete and accurate reporting of studies of diagnostic accuracy: The STARD Initiative. *Ann Intern Med*. 2003;138(1):40–44.

Chapter 6

Safety Evaluation

The introduction of electronic medical records (EMRs) and other electronic software tools to healthcare has brought great benefits to patients and providers. Technology can be beneficial: for example, computerized physician order entry (CPOE) can substantially decrease the number of medication errors,[1] and barcode technologies can significantly decrease the number of medication dispensing errors.[2] On the other hand, technologies could be harmful. For example, CPOE implementation has been associated with the increased mortality of pediatric patients.[3] As human-designed-and-built elements, electronic tools have the potential to introduce new problems. Unfortunately, they can also magnify existing problems and introduce risks.

The Washington Patient Safety Coalition (WPSC) commissioned a report to enhance patient safety by identifying electronic health record (EHR)-related risks and ways of mitigating them.

The problem specification had to define the problem that was to be solved and the constraints that an acceptable solution had to satisfy.

As outlined in Chapter 2, the first step in healthcare information technology (HIT or health IT) evaluation involves answering the following question: Is the technology safe? This concerns the safety of the technology and the actions originating from its use. As a broad comparison, this step could be considered to be similar to Phase I in clinical trials, when investigators assess the safety of new interventions. Also, safety assessments are not always transferable to new clinical situations. Only post-implementation surveillance studies (such as Phase IV of clinical trials) can generate knowledge regarding safety. Safety assessment should be performed as an initial requirement to demonstrate that technology has been developed (manufactured) to a standard that will not render it, in itself, a risk to patients and users. HIT systems designed to directly improve patient outcomes (such as clinical decision support [CDS] or EMR) must be rigorously evaluated using this step. However, there are currently *no regulatory requirements for evaluating HIT system safety*, though these systems are known to directly affect patient care in both positive and negative ways.

6.1 Role of Government Organizations in HIT Safety Evaluation

The government has recognized that if health IT systems are not designed and used correctly, they can introduce new risks in addition to their expected benefits. Two organizations, the Office of the National Coordinator for Health IT (ONC) and the Agency for Healthcare Research and Quality (AHRQ), have held regular meetings to coordinate activities related to research and reporting on health IT and patient safety. Two other organizations with oversight are the Centers for Medicare and Medicaid Services (CMS) and the Food and Drug Administration (FDA). Moreover, a number of public and private stakeholders exist. For example, the AHRQ website listed 88 patient safety organizations that have demonstrated interest in health IT.

In 2011, the Institute of Medicine (IOM) summarized the existing knowledge regarding the effects of health IT on patient safety, publishing it in the report, "Health IT and Patient Safety: Building Safer Systems for Better Care"[4] (available to download as a free PDF ebook at http://iom.nationalacademies.org/Reports/2011/Health-IT-and-Patient-Safety-Building-Safer-Systems-for-Better-Care.aspx). One of the key findings was that health IT could improve patient safety in areas such as medication safety. However, there were significant gaps in the literature regarding how health IT impacted patient safety overall. Based on this report, the ONC developed the U.S. Department of Health and Human Services (HHS) Health IT Safety Plan, which included two objectives:

1. To use health IT to make care safer
2. To continuously improve the safety of health IT

Furthermore, some recommendations were as follows:

1. That research on measures specifically related to the design, implementation, usability, and safe use of health IT by all users be expanded.
2. That standardized testing procedures be expanded and the post-deployment safety testing of EHRs be promoted.
3. That new methods for measuring the impact of health IT on safety be developed.
4. That the secretary of the HHS recommends that Congress establish an independent federal entity for investigating patient safety deaths, serious injuries, or potentially unsafe conditions associated with health IT.
5. That, if progress toward safety and reliability is not sufficient (as determined by the secretary), the secretary directs the FDA to exercise all available authority to regulate EHRs, health information exchanges, and personal health records (PHRs).

The Food and Drug Administration Safety and Innovation Act (FDASIA) of 2012 was signed into law in July 2012. It requires the HHS secretary, "acting through the Commissioner of FDA, and in consultation with the National Coordinator for HIT and the Chairman of FCC," to post a report within 18 months that "contains a proposed strategy and recommendations on an appropriate, risk-based regulatory framework pertaining to health information technology, including mobile medical applications, that promotes innovation, protects patient safety, and avoids regulatory duplication." However, there is still no clarity regarding how exactly the safety of HITs should be tested and reported.

The FDA regulates medical device space, which it partially defines as follows: "A device is an instrument, apparatus, implement, machine, contrivance, implant, in vitro reagent, or other similar or related article, including a component part, or accessory which is intended for use in the diagnosis of disease or other conditions, or in the cure, mitigation, treatment, or prevention of disease, in man or other animals." Modern decision support systems and EMR pretty much fall under the definition of "software devices." However, over the years, they have continued to be a "gray area" that does not require mandatory FDA approval. The current regulatory proceeds are presented in Figure 6.1.

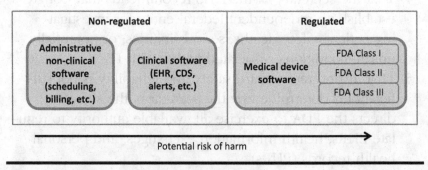

Figure 6.1 Current regulatory space for HIT.

ONC EHR Technology Certification Program

The ONC Health IT Certification Program was started in 2012. It is a *voluntary certification program* that the ONC established to provide for the certification of health IT standards, implementation specifications, and certification criteria that the secretary adopted. The ONC Health IT Certification Program supports the availability of certified health IT for its recommended and required users under other federal, state, and private programs. Moreover, it provides a defined process to ensure that (EHR) technologies meet the adopted standards and certification criteria to help providers and hospitals achieve the meaningful use (MU) objectives and measures that the CMS established (https://www.healthit.gov/policy-researchers-implementers/onc-health-it-certification-program). One of the test procedures (§170.314 (g) (3) Safety-enhanced design) concerns safety health IT products and especially concerns user-centered design (UCD).

Meaningful Use (Stage 2) and 2014 Edition Standards and Certification Criteria

Stage 2 of MU took effect in 2014 and specifies two safety-enhanced certification criteria that require developers to publicly identify a method of ensuring UCD and an approach to quality management.

Safety Evaluation outside the Legislative Process

As vendors are exempt from liability, the burden of safety evaluation would be the responsibility of healthcare organizations. They would have to analyze and track the impact of HIT use on patient safety. As a broader objective, EMR and related technologies should not do additional harm and clinical practice should perform at least as before without new technology. That is ultimately the responsibility of IT implementers, ongoing support service, and technology users.

Technology-related safety problems can be divided into two major groups:

1. Computer-related and technical issues
2. Human–computer interaction–related issues

Computer-related and technical issues can be grouped into two major categories: (1) system availability and (2) malfunctions. Specific examples include the following:

■ Slowing or going down of the network, causing delays in the ability to retrieve data
■ Instability of software due to programming errors and bugs
■ Unreliable hardware or software platforms
■ Lost data
■ Interface failure between different clinical systems
■ Data not displaying properly in the system (wrong record retrieved)
■ Unauthorized access due to criminal intent

Human–computer interaction issues can be grouped into two major categories: (1) interaction with the system and (2) incorrect use. Specific examples include the following:

■ System's failure to meet the needs of clinicians
■ Poor usability, failing to alert the user properly
■ Ignoring the alert by the user or its being overridden
■ Entering clinical information into the wrong record
■ Incorrect entry of data into the electronic record
■ Failure to enter data into the system at all
■ Incomplete data entry and/or non-entry of data
■ Working of the system in one context or organization but it is unsafe or failed in another
■ Changing the routine clinical workflow system, introducing new potential error pathways

6.2 Problem Identification and Related Metrics: What Should One Study?

Both technical and human–computer interaction issues can result in errors that negatively affect the care delivery process. However, not only could lack of training and experience contribute to errors. Incorrect use could also quite often indicate and be mitigated by product flaws. Providers work under pressure, and system design flaws such as poorly engineered systems, lack of workflow standardization, and ineffective data presentation can encourage the development of safety problems.

Safety evaluation should address technology and the processes in which the technology is used. Some degree of technology evaluation is often required. However, technology use is not possible until after many years of clinical use (similar to Phase IV of clinical trials). It is also important to evaluate safety when technology is not used.

The specific study design will depend on the question that the evaluator is attempting to answer. At first glance, it is obvious that the question will be "Does this specific HIT cause patient harm?" Harm could be measured as the rate of unintended complications based on the specific use case of technology.

Patient engagement tools could concern the following:

- Dealing with the reliability of data that patients and their families enter.
- Testing against unauthorized access is an essential element of any computer system development, but from the perspective of safety evaluation, the question is "How could unauthorized access affect patient management?" For example, could a diabetic patient have the wrong dosage entered into his or her home medication list?

CPOE systems could be tested for the following safety concerns:

- Time from the decision to actual entry in the system (How would this impact the care process?)
- A templated, inflexible data entry form's introduction of incorrect or partial orders
- Double dosing
- Drug–drug interaction problems
- Clinical disruption
- Wrong patient orders

CDS systems and smart clinical alerts—"sniffers"—could be evaluated on the basis of

- Their diagnostic performance (sensitivity and specificity)
- The quality of detection compared to other routine methods or other systems
- The acceptance rate of alerts or suggestions
- Their override rate
- Their rate of adherence to protocol

Barcoding technologies can also introduce safety issues, such as

- A scan barcode attached to the wrong patient.
- Failure at visual confirmation of the correct patient, intended medication, and dosage.
- Multiple simultaneous scans (e.g., due to poor usability) and subsequent dealing with dispensing.

Other HIT-related metrics could include the following:

- System uptime
- System response and start time
- Incorrect reports of diagnostic or laboratory tests

■ Changes in standard performance metrics after system implementation

HIT technologies are complex systems. Studying them as a whole reveals that many factors apart from broken technology could introduce safety issues. These include an inappropriate workflow process, the influence of organizations and external agencies, as well as users of technology (training, motivation, burnout).

Where Can One Study the Safety Evaluation of HIT? Passive and Active Evaluation

An initial scientific-based safety evaluation is very similar in intention to a Phase I clinical trial. It involves researchers taking technology to the "laboratory" setting and using a small sample size to identify critical barriers to moving technology into a real "live" setting. The "laboratory" is not a traditional bench/wet laboratory. In clinical informatics, a laboratory could be any closed office space or room with computers connected to a hospital network that could simulate a work environment. Such a room should be located close to or on the hospital floor with clinicians and patients (improving convenience and increasing participation). The ideal clinical informatics laboratory is a repurposed standard patient room and could be used for a number of activities, for instance, interviews and the simulation of workflow processes (Figure 6.2).

Evaluating HIT safety requires the performance of studies on the safety of the technology and of the processes it is used in. Legislation often requires the first for FDA Class I, II, III devices. The second cannot happen until the real clinical evaluation phase, when it is safe to use the technology in real clinical situations and for patient care. The safety studies are mostly similar in intention to a Phase IV clinical trial and can only be done after the implementation of the technology. It is also important to

Figure 6.2   Clinical informatics laboratory in the form of a repurposed patient room. (a) Hospital floor. (b) Interview station. (c) Eye tracking device station. (d) Standard workstation for observation.

evaluate the danger of not using HITs at all (uncertainty in diagnosis or therapy without the use of a decision support system).

Safety evaluation could involve two types of studies: passive observation and active tests. Both can be used in "lab" settings and "live" settings. Passive observation and evaluation is mostly used to study a system after going "live." During that time, evaluators collect data using the observation methodology to identify any unintended consequences of system implementation. The most appropriate designs for this type of study are prospective cohort and before-after studies. Active tests in the context of safety evaluation studies could be pre-implementation laboratory-based studies that are designed to actively identify problems with the system studied at the pre-production stage and during prototype development. A number of study designs could be used based on the factors being studied. Diagnostic studies, a variety of surveys, and usability techniques could be used (Figure 6.3).

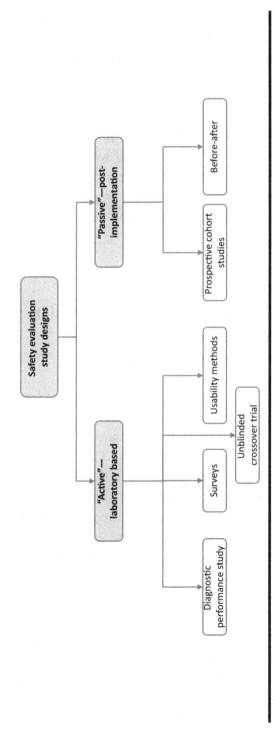

Figure 6.3   Evaluation study designs to address the clinical safety of HIT.

The majority of randomized controlled trials concerning the technologies could be unethical in a live clinical environment. If, for example, a system detected a live threatening situation such as sepsis, it would be unethical to be aware of this and not notify the provider of the need to take action. That scenario could be undertaken in a laboratory setting as a parallel "silent" test. It is also important to remember that, in most studies involving technology, blinding would be impossible. For the study of HIT systems and their impact, more feasible designs, such as unblinded crossover trials, should be utilized. Other typical HIT safety problems and potential evaluation studies are presented in Table 6.1.

6.3 Tools and Methodologies to Assist Capture and Report HIT Safety Events: Passive Evaluation

Two documents may be used as a starting point for the development of a HIT safety evaluation program. One is a publication from AHRQ—the "Health IT Hazard Manager Beta-Test: Final Report."[5] Another publication is "The SAFER Guides: Empowering organizations to improve the safety and effectiveness of electronic health records."[6] The Health IT Hazard Manager tool supports the characterization and communication of hazards and their potential and actual adverse effects. Such a tool would support the creation of consistent, comparable information and shared learning about hazards associated with the following:

1. A specific health IT application (vendor product)
2. A type of application (e.g., all pharmacy order-management applications)
3. A specific combination of application types (e.g., pharmacy order management and order entry)

Table 6.1 Safety Problems, Factors, Manifestations, and Potential Evaluation Studies Designed to Address Them

Safety Problems	Factors	Manifestations	Evaluation Studies
System malfunction	Hardware defects and software bugs	Failure to alert Missing, incorrect data	Technical evaluation Diagnostic performance study—comparison with original system—gold standard
	Inappropriate access to system	System misuse	Penetration test
System availability	Scheduled system maintenance Unexpected outages		Technical evaluation
	Weak infrastructure		Technical evaluation
Incorrect use	Poor workflow design	Selection workflow Workaround	Usability studies Surveys
	Visual design flaw	Alert fatigue Information overload	Cognitive testing Usability studies Surveys
	Inadequate training	Errors in usage	Simulation studies
Interaction with system	Functionality gap	Limited functionality	Usability studies
	User resistance	Unreliable usage and transfer of data	Surveys Observational study

As Figure 6.4 illustrates, hazards may arise due to inadequacies in the design, manufacture, implementation, or maintenance of health IT. They may also arise in the interactions between health IT and other complex healthcare systems (e.g., the coordination of a patient's post-discharge medication list among hospital physicians, community pharmacies, and outpatient physicians). If hazards are identified and eliminated before an application is implemented (represented by the grayed oval in Figure 6.4), no adverse effect can occur. If, however, the hazard is not identified or cannot be completely eliminated, there is a risk that it will compromise care—especially in the case of a fully automated system that users cannot override.

Proactive hazard control has many advantages. Compared to a limited focus on safety incidents, proactive hazard control has a more systematic approach to the full range of hazards that health IT may create. Second, instead of typically focusing on "user error," proactive hazard control concentrates on how health IT vendors, implementers, supporters, and clinicians unknowingly create hazards. Proactive hazard control also reduces biases associated with retrospective analysis as well as sponsor and confirmation biases. The Health IT Hazard Manager is designed to be operated on a secure, private web application. Each care delivery organization (CDO) and every individual user from that organization must register prior to using the Hazard Manager.

The SAFER Guides (http://www.healthit.gov/safer/) are designed to help healthcare organizations conduct self-assessments to optimize the safety and safe use of EHRs in the following areas:

1. High priority practices
2. Organizational responsibilities
3. Contingency planning
4. System configuration
5. System interfaces

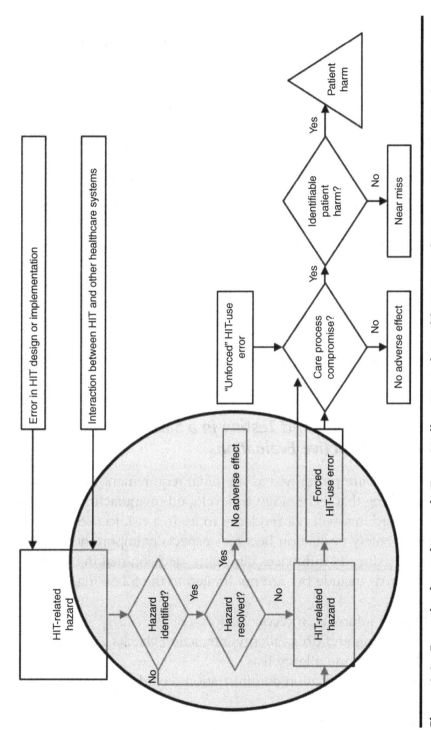

Figure 6.4 Proactive hazard control. (From Walker JM et al. Health IT Hazard Manager Beta-Test: Final Report. AHRQ Publication No. 12-0058-EF. Public domain.)

6. Patient identification
7. Computerized provider order entry with decision support
8. Test result reporting and follow-up
9. Clinician communication

Each of the nine SAFER Guides begins with a checklist of "recommended practices." The downloadable SAFER Guides provide fillable circles that can be used to indicate the extent to which each recommended practice has been implemented. The SAFER Guides are based on the best evidence available at the time (2013), including a literature review, an expert opinion, and field testing at a wide range of healthcare organizations (ranging from small ambulatory practices to large health systems).

It is important to understand that safety evaluation results are not always transferable to other clinical settings and scenarios. Information on safety in new clinical situations can only be generated through post-implementation surveillance studies.

Simulation Studies and Testing in a Safe Environment: Active Evaluations

Safety studies are performed as an initial requirement for demonstrating that technology is developed (manufactured) to a standard that will not render it, in itself, a risk to users (patients). Safety evaluation becomes especially important if technology directly influences clinicians' decision making. The relevant areas include but are not limited to the following:

1. Clinical information reconciliation
2. Drug–drug and drug–allergy interaction checks
3. Medication and allergy lists
4. Electronic medication administration record in inpatient settings
5. Clinical decision support

6. Computerized provider order entry
7. Electronic prescribing

After the initial development of new technology, it would be good practice to use the test procedures described in the ONC document, "Test Procedure for §170.314(g)(3) Safety-Enhanced Design," for reporting. The document is used for the ONC certification process and originated from "NISTIR 7742 Customized Common Industry Format Template for Electronic Health Record Usability Testing" (http://www.nist.gov/manuscript-publication-search.cfm?pub_id=907312). It is customized for use in EMR usability testing, modified from software engineering—Software product Quality Requirements and Evaluation (SQuaRE) Common Industry Format (CIF) for usability test reports (ISO/IEC 25062:2006(E)).

As we outlined, laboratory studies could use a number of methodologies and metrics for evaluation. A number of published manuscripts in peer-reviewed literature could be used as methodological examples. The "Participation in EHR-based Simulation Improves Recognition of Patient Safety Issues" study[7] used a simulated EHR environment with 2 intensive care unit (ICU) cases and 14 safety issues for each one.[8] Participants in the study included residents, who were given 10 min to review a case and then present management changes. Participants received an immediate debriefing regarding missed issues and strategies for data gathering in the EHR. The study showed that 38 participants had an average error recognition rate of 41%. This type of study in the simulation environment allows the identification of poorly designed electronic tools in the early stages and the taking of appropriate action to redesign them. Importantly, since its laboratory testing is isolated from the patient care electronic environment, there is no potential harm to human subjects.

Another example of a pre-implementation HIT safety evaluation study in the laboratory setting was published in the journal, *Critical Care Medicine*. "The Effect of Two Different Electronic

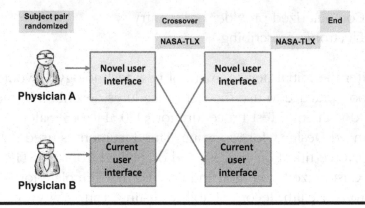

Figure 6.5 Schematic representation of crossover study design in laboratory setting.

Health Record User Interfaces on Intensive Care Provider Task Load, Errors of Cognition, and Performance" was a crossover study. Physicians, randomly assigned to either a standard EMR or a novel user interface, were asked to perform a structured task.[9] The task required providers to use the assigned electronic environment to review the medical records of ICU patients and to answer clinical questions posed in the form of a structured questionnaire. The primary outcome was the task load, measured using the NASA-task load index (NASA-TLX). Secondary outcome measures included time-to-task completion, the number of errors of cognition measured by comparing the subject to post hoc gold standard questionnaire responses, and the quantity of information that each environment presented to subjects. As a crossover study, each physician experienced each EMR environment (Figure 6.5).

Since data and sample are not normally distributed, non-parametric methods were used.

6.4 Summary

Currently, there are no regulatory requirements for evaluating HIT system safety, even if systems are directly used in patient care and may affect it in a negative way. Systems could be developed from erroneous specifications, have programming errors and bugs, use unreliable hardware or software platforms, or work correctly in a specific setting but be unsafe or fail in another, changing the routine and workflow and introducing new potential failure points. It is good practice to evaluate HIT safety in the pre-implementation and post-implementation periods.

Suggested Reading

An oversight framework for assuring patient safety in health information technology. http://bipartisanpolicy.org/library/ oversight-framework-assuring-patient-safety-health-information- technology/.

Committee on Patient Safety and Health Information Technology, and Board on Health Care Services. 2012. *Health IT and Patient Safety: Building Safer Systems for Better Care*. Washington, DC: National Academies Press. ISBN: 978- 0309221122. (Free ebook: http://www.nap.edu/catalog/13269/ health-it-and-patient-safety-building-safer-systems-for-better.)

Harrington L, Kennerly D, Johnson C. Safety issues related to the electronic medical record (EMR): Synthesis of the literature from the last decade, 2000–2009. *J Healthc Manag*. 56(1):31–43; PMID: 21323026.

HealthIT.gov safety resource. http://www.healthit.gov/ policy-researchers-implementers/health-it-and-safety.

Health IT Safety Program: Progress on Health IT Patient Safety Action and Surveillance Plan. https://www.healthit.gov/sites/ default/files/ONC_HIT_SafetyProgramReport_9-9-14_.pdf.

Walker JM, Carayon P, Leveson N, et al. EHR safety: The way forward to safe and effective systems. *J Am Med Inform Assoc*. 15(3):272–277. PMID: 18308981.

References

1. Bates DW, Teich JM, Lee J, et al. The impact of computerized physician order entry on medication error prevention. *J Am*

Med Inform Assoc. 6(4):313–321. http://www.ncbi.nlm.nih.gov/pubmed/10428004.

2. Poon EG, Cina JL, Churchill W, et al. Medication dispensing errors and potential adverse drug events before and after implementing bar code technology in the pharmacy. *Ann Intern Med*. 2006;145(6):426–434. http://www.ncbi.nlm.nih.gov/pubmed/16983130.

3. Han YY, Carcillo JA, Venkataraman ST, et al. Unexpected increased mortality after implementation of a commercially sold computerized physician order entry system. *Pediatrics*. 2005;116(6):1506–1512.

4. Committee on Patient Safety and Health Information Technology, and Board on Health Care Services. 2012. *Health IT and Patient Safety: Building Safer Systems for Better Care*. Washington, DC: National Academies Press.

5. Walker JM, Hassol A, Bradshaw B, Rezaee ME. Health IT hazard manager beta-test: Final report. (Prepared by Abt Associates and Geisinger Health System, under Contract No. HHSA290200600011i, #14.) AHRQ Publication No. 12-0058-EF. Rockville, MD: Agency for Health Care Research and Quality.

6. Sittig DF, Ash JS, Singh H. The SAFER guides: Empowering organizations to improve the safety and effectiveness of electronic health records. *Am J Manag Care*. 2014;20(5):418–423. http://www.ncbi.nlm.nih.gov/pubmed/25181570.

7. Stephenson LS, Gorsuch A, Hersh WR, Mohan V, Gold JA. Participation in EHR based simulation improves recognition of patient safety issues. *BMC Med Educ*. 2014;14:224.

8. March CA, Steiger D, Scholl G, Mohan V, Hersh WR, Gold JA. Use of simulation to assess electronic health record safety in the intensive care unit: A pilot study. *BMJ Open*. 2013;3(4):4e002549. doi:10.1136/bmjopen-2013-002549.

9. Ahmed A, Chandra S, Herasevich V, Gajic O, Pickering BW. The effect of two different electronic health record user interfaces on intensive care provider task load, errors of cognition, and performance. *Crit Care Med*. 2011;39(7):1626–1634.

Chapter 7

Cost Evaluation

Regardless of the healthcare model—private, nonprofit, or government supported—an entity always pays the bills, such as the cost of facilities, supplies, salaries, and other expenses. Healthcare information technology (HIT or health IT) has value in decision making for purchases and informed decisions in general. It makes cost analysis an important part of the evaluation process. The magnitude of cost evaluation could vary based on the technology and implementation goals.

Most HIT cost analysis concerns customer decision making (i.e., the purchaser of technology). Executives eventually approve the purchase of a technological product. These can be complex, expensive devices such as computer tomography machines or the project of wiring a hospital floor with bedside monitors. Increased consumer health products such as wearable devices and mobile phone applications mean that patients will be another group of customers who are interested in the (primarily indirect) financial benefit.

Modern research and development is expensive and the software market is growing, so software technologies rarely evaluate cost against benefit adequately before implementation. When they do, it's usually about easy-to-measure metrics and short-term benefit, not complex metrics pertinent to the whole healthcare system and society.

Innovation in healthcare doesn't often start with direct financial benefit in mind. In most situations, it targets an existing clinical problem. However, adequately measuring the financial implication of technology is important in building a complete picture of HIT. The following steps should be taken before any actual financial evaluation:

1. Understand how HIT products will produce value.
2. Know who will be the main stakeholders to benefit from those products.
3. Outline associated costs and the potential generated value of technology.
4. Do a cost estimation based on the best available background information and assumptions.
5. Choose the best cost evaluation method.
6. Perform a study with sensitivity analysis to calculate variation in estimation.

Doing these steps in the early stages of technology development could help to avoid critical pitfalls or correct them sooner rather than later. Cost evaluation information will also advantageously position technology proponents to obtain stakeholders' support.

Economic evaluation guides the decision-making process in HIT by comparing alternatives or no intervention with respect to resource utilization and expected outcome. The outcomes could be valued in monetary units or in clinical units, such as quality-adjusted life years (QALYs).

Cost is important in decision making about technology implementation and usage, so we must understand the rationale and constraints in decision making. Administrative decision-making costs play a key role in efficiency, but they aren't the only factor. For clinicians, the associated cost of decision making plays a less significant role if other components of technology have a satisfactory performance (Figure 7.1).

Once the healthcare technology system is implemented, it has ongoing maintenance costs that are more obvious and evident to administrators.

The resources of the world are limited, and medicine has economic considerations for using one or another technique or device. The economic evaluation addresses the cost not only of improving quality of life and increasing age, but also of implementing diagnostic and therapeutic interventions, including HIT.

7.1 Health Economics Basics

Measuring cost is sometimes challenging. Cost of service is not the only customer charge, and sometimes the total bill isn't collected. The healthcare billing process includes a reimbursement process, and the whole process could be timely with charges adjusted for inflation. As many other components and indirect expenses influence healthcare economics, an analysis of HIT efficiency should be diverse, comprehensive, and evaluated in financial and nonfinancial terms. In HIT, it should include training costs, for example. Other costs, such as implementation labor costs, can be extrapolated to financial terms.

From the point of view of a single healthcare organization, important benefits are usually short term; long-term benefits are more important to society but don't always represent the immediate interests of a single institution. However, the impact of HIT at society level should be evaluated as well.

Several main types of cost analysis can be applied to HIT:

1. *Cost benefit analysis* (CBA): Costs are the monetary value of changed health outcomes to produce financial gain or loss. CBA compares costs and benefits, which are quantified in common monetary units. *Cost-consequence*

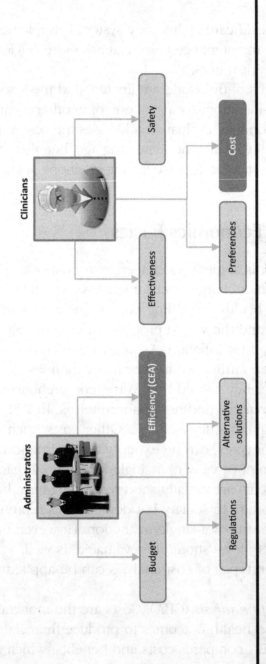

Figure 7.1 Components of decision making for administrators and clinicians.

analysis (CCA) is a form of CBA that uses different units for costs and benefits; different types of benefits don't use the same units for outcome measurements and don't combine them in a single unit.

2. *Cost-effectiveness analysis* (CEA): The monetary cost relates to changes in an important health outcome as producing a cost-effectiveness ratio (cost-per-unit outcome). CEA compares costs in monetary units with outcomes in quantitative nonmonetary units (e.g., reduced mortality or morbidity). *Cost-utility analysis* (CUA) is a form of CEA that compares costs in monetary units with outcomes in terms of their utility to the patient, usually QALYs.

3. *Cost-minimization analysis* (CMA): This analysis of technology replaces a current or alternative system and is equally effective in providing equal benefit at lower cost. In other words, CMA determines the least costly among alternative interventions that are assumed to produce equivalent outcomes.

4. *Return on investment* (ROI): This economic analysis determines the potential gain or loss from investment by simply dividing earnings by investment.

Setting and Methodology

As shown in the previous list, the main types of economic analysis don't require a specially designed experiment, because they analyze collected data from technology implementation or computer modeling based on actual data and/or assumptions. No laboratory experiment is needed for a financial analysis of HIT.

The evaluator is required to have comprehensive access to technology information (log files) and financial documents. Access to library and research databases is a plus for compiling historical information, assumptions, and experience outside the organization.

During economic evaluation, study investigators should pay attention to the key elements in Table 7.1.

Table 7.1 Key Elements in Economic Evaluation Study

Group	Step	Element	Process
Study design	1	Study question	State the economic importance of the topic and study from the viewpoint of stakeholders (patients, clinicians, payers, hospitals, etc.).
	2	Selection of alternative options	Describe the problem, intervention, and alternative intervention. Justify selection.
	3	Type of economic evaluation	State what type of economic evaluation is used and justify its selection in relation to the study question.
Data collection	4	Effectiveness data (clinical outcome)	Provide details on study design, method of data synthesis, or modeling methodology, if used.
	5	Benefit measurement and valuation	State the primary outcome measure. Describe the methodology used for health benefits. Describe indirect benefits, if measured, and describe their relevance to the study question.
	6	Cost measurement	Describe the provenance of data cost. Detail the methods of estimating resources and unit costs. Provide details on adjustments for inflation, currency conversion, etc.

(Continued)

Table 7.1 (Continued)   Key Elements in Economic Evaluation Study

Group	Step	Element	Process
	7	Modeling	If modeling is used, justify its selection and parameters.
Analysis and interpretation	8	Timing adjustments for outcomes and costs	State study time frame and any discounts for a long study.
	9	Allowance for uncertainty	Provide details on the statistical test used. If a sensitivity analysis is performed, detail the approach used.
	10	Presentation of results	Provide the answer to the main study question. Provide the outcomes and data costs separately before combining.

Source: Based on McLaughlin, N. et al., *Neurosurg Focus*, 37(5), E2, 2014.[1]

What to Measure and Outcomes

Complex financial analysis requires deep understanding of economic principles and should be performed by economic professionals. Understanding its basis will help in planning and designing the evaluation.

The total cost of technology can be divided into two parts: fixed cost ("hard" dollars) and variable cost ("soft" dollars). Both can be affected by a new HIT product, but the impact vectors are different. As a first important starting point for evaluation, all possible costs should be identified. The second and third steps will identify all relevant ranges of cost and methods of measurement (Figure 7.2).

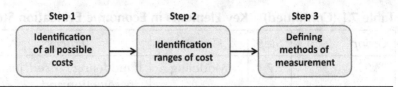

Figure 7.2 Basic steps in financial evaluation.

Table 7.2 Main Group of Economic-Related Metrics That Could Be Used in HIT Evaluation

Metric	Example
Capacity	Freeing up staff and facility could increase patient flow.
External services	Contracts for services and maintenance with outside organizations. Custom software development.
Human resources	Full-time equivalent reduction or avoidance, project effort reduction to increase efficiency. Project management cost. Training cost. Help desk cost.
Infrastructure	Equipment and software cost. Space and remodeling. Reducing cost ownership of existing technologies. IT security cost.
Patient-related impact	Length of stay (LOS) and readmissions. Patient safety events, including adverse drug events (ADE). Disease prevention.
Revenue	Direct impact on reimbursement. Increased revenue due to better capacity or efficiency. Reduction of reimbursement denials. Audit cost.
Supplies	Changes in equipment demand or day-to-day supplies.

The outcome measurement of the financial impact of HIT is the same as other interventions and can be divided into the general categories shown in Table 7.2.

Eliminating waste, improving productivity, and reducing length of hospital stay are considered the main general outcomes of cost evaluation.

Fixed-cost savings supported by evidence have a definite and quantifiable effect on cash flow in the near term. Cost reductions and decreased length of hospital stay could be considered "hard" outcomes. Variable cost savings originate from process improvement and increase capacity and productivity without reducing staff, and they lower malpractice expenses and avoid future costs. High-quality economic evaluation of technologies should include the following six key components[2]:

1. Explain a perspective
2. Include options for comparison
3. Define a time frame
4. Establish costs
5. Define and calculate impact on outcomes
6. Compare costs and outcomes for each option

7.2 Main Types of Cost Analysis Applied to HIT

We have defined the main types of economic evaluation, and one of the critical initial steps in HIT economic evaluation is selecting the appropriate type of analysis.

Cost-Benefit Analysis

CBA is an economic evaluation in which all costs and consequences of a program are expressed in the same units, usually money. It is used to determine allocative efficiency, such as comparing costs and benefits across programs serving different patient groups.

Cost measurement: Monetary units.

Outcome measurement: Monetary unit attributed to health effects. Benefit–cost ratio.

Limitations: A key role that this type of study plays is a hypothetical estimation of cost and introduces limitations to reflect real-life economic benefits. Qualitative variables such as improvements in patient safety are not easy to convert to monetary units, which is important in healthcare.

Items considered in HIT cost evaluation: Introducing new technology creates additional costs that don't exist in a non-technological environment, such as system infrastructure, application, and support.

Data preparation: The first step in CBA is to tabulate items that need to be included in the calculation (Table 7.3).

Data sources: In a direct cost-benefit study, the best data source to calculate financial value is accounting records. The better accuracy benefits should be adjusted for inflation if the comparison covers many years.

An example of a published study on CBA of electronic medical record (EMR) implementation is "Cost-Benefit Analysis of Electronic Medical Record System at a Tertiary Care Hospital" published by Samsung Medical Center investigators from Korea.[3]

CCA is a form of CBA that uses different units for costs and benefits; different benefits don't use the same units for outcome measurements and don't combine them in a single unit. This is different from CEA, as outlined in the next section. In CCA, different decision makers use their own weights on the different benefits and on costs. CCA is of more interest to public health.[4]

Cost-Effectiveness Analysis

CEA is an economic evaluation in which the costs and consequences of alternative interventions are expressed in cost per

Table 7.3 Variables to Estimate and Include in CBA Interventions

	Item	Old System	New System
Cost			
Benefit			
Additional revenue			

unit of health outcome. CEA is used to determine technical efficiency in, for example, comparing the costs and consequences of competing interventions for a given patient group within a given budget.

Cost measurement: Monetary unit.

Outcome measurement: Any disease-specific, nonmonetary natural unit. The cost-effectiveness ratio is calculated as the cost of a new intervention divided by health benefit units (e.g., adverse drug events).

Limitations: Cost-effectiveness is incremental; added costs need to be addressed appropriately when compared with a control group. Two articles in the references give broad perspectives on the limitations of CEA.[5,6]

Data preparation: It is critical to describe the intervention accurately using all information essential to interpreting the estimated costs and benefits. Collected data should be tabulated.

Data sources: This type of study could use accounting data and public data. Data from the literature can help estimate the potential effectiveness of technology before its purchase and implementation.

CEA is an effective and important tool to use before any major HIT development and adoption. A good overview publication is "A Clinician's Guide to Cost-Effectiveness Analysis," published in 1990.[7] The Canadian study "Cost-Effectiveness of an Electronic Medication Ordering and Administration System in Reducing Adverse Drug Events" used CEA to investigate the cost of introducing an electronic medication-ordering system and its potential impact on reducing adverse drug events.[8] CUA is a form of economic study design in which interventions produce different consequences in terms of both quantity and quality of life, which are expressed as *utilities*. These measures comprise both length of life and subjective levels of well-being. The best-known utility measure is the QALY, a unit of measure of utility that combines life years gained as a result of health interventions. Defined by the World Bank as a "common measure of health improvement used in cost-utility analysis, it measures life expectancy adjusted for quality of life."

Outcome measurement: Utility score (nonmonetary). Cost measurement: Monetary unit.

An example of CUA that uses the modeling approach is the UK article "Modeling the Expected Net Benefits of Interventions to Reduce the Burden of Medication Errors."[9]

Cost-Minimization Analysis

CMA is an economic evaluation in which the consequences of competing interventions are the same and in which only inputs (i.e., costs) are taken into consideration. The aim of CMA is to determine the least costly alternative therapy to achieve the same outcome.

Outcome measurement varies but is equal among alternatives.

Cost measurement: Monetary unit.

Cost minimization can only be used to compare two systems that could be comparable in end effect on the patient outcome. This method is very useful for comparing an old HIT system with a new system assumed to have the same performance or impact. There is often no reliable evidence between two products to demonstrate their equivalence, and if equivalence cannot be demonstrated, CMA is inappropriate.

An example of CMA in HIT is the article "Cost-Effectiveness of Telemonitoring for High-Risk Pregnant Women."[10] In this retrospective study, telemonitoring of high-risk pregnant women was compared to hospitalization for monitoring. ICD9CM codes were used to identify patients' cohort for study, and possible scenarios and costs were estimated based on hospital length-of-stay (LOS) associated cost. For the telemonitoring group, the associated operational cost was estimated, and using those assumptions and numbers, potential cost reduction was calculated. Such a study has limitations, as many nonmonetary factors cannot be taken into account (e.g., the patient's educational level, as it is needed to use home telemonitoring system, psychological condition, willingness to perform telemonitoring, distance from hospital to travel in case of emergency, and the clinical condition itself).

However, such types of studies can roughly estimate the cost reduction with new technology introduction.

Return on Investment

The traditional financial definition of ROI is simply earnings divided by investment.

The definition of earnings and cost over time in a big HIT implementation project, however, is not straightforward. Various tangible/intangible costs and direct/indirect benefits must be considered during analysis.

Cost measurement: Monetary unit.

Outcome measurement: ROI calculation = (estimated lifetime benefit − estimated lifetime costs)/estimated lifetime costs.

Benefits measurements: Not always in monetary units; sometimes distant and fairly indirect (e.g., staff time saved or potential savings from decreased errors).

When the cost of a big HIT implementation project is estimated, it usually breaks into the following categories:

- Electronic medical records
- Computerized provider order entry
- Decision support
- Dashboards and results reporting
- Knowledge retrieval systems
- Consumer portals and related technologies
- Mobile computing
- Telemedicine
- Communication and data exchange
- Revenue cycle system
- Analytics and datamarts

An example of ROI analysis reporting is the article "Modeling Return on Investment for an Electronic Medical Record system in Lilongwe, Malawi."[11] This study aimed to model the financial effects of implementing a hospital-wide EMR in a tertiary medical center. In this modeling study, the authors collected data on expenditures with the paper-based (pre-EMR) system and then estimated reductions based on EMR system information from the United States adjusted by ambulatory data from low-income settings. The study targeted three impact areas: length of stay, transcription time, and laboratory use.

The ROI was calculated on a five-year time frame.

Many such studies involve estimations, so it is important to carry out a sensitivity analysis and list all limitations.

The traditional business-case values focus on reducing costs. In HIT, however, more and more quality becomes the important component. Estimating the ROI for health IT systems may include "hard" benefits (decreased length of stay) or "soft" benefits (improved patient safety and quality from misinterpreting handwritten notes). Hard benefits are usually measured in terms of revenue, whereas most soft benefits are difficult to quantify. Use of traditional ROI in HIT should be limited and when possible should be replaced by other types of financial analyses.

How to Report Economic Evaluation Studies

The Consolidated Health Economic Evaluation Reporting Standards (CHEERS) statement consolidates previous health economic evaluation guidelines efforts into one current, useful reporting guide.[12]

Compared with epidemiology-based clinical studies that target intervention reports, economic reports include additional items, such as resource use and costs (see Table 7.4).

**Table 7.4   CHEERS Checklist Lists Items to Include When
Reporting Economic Evaluations of Health**

Section/Item	Item No.	Recommendation
Title and abstract		
Title	1	Identify the study as an economic evaluation or use more specific terms, such as "cost-effectiveness analysis," and describe the interventions compared.
Abstract	2	Provide a structured summary of objectives, perspective, setting, methods (including study design and inputs), results (including base case and uncertainty analyses), and conclusions.
Introduction		
Background and objectives	3	Provide an explicit statement of the broader context for the study.
		Present the study question and its relevance for health policy or practice decisions.
Methods		
Target population and subgroups	4	Describe the characteristics of the base case population and subgroups analyzed, including why they were chosen.
Setting and location	5	State relevant aspects of the system(s) in which the decision(s) need(s) to be made.
Study perspective	6	Describe the perspective of the study and relate this to the costs being evaluated.
Comparators	7	Describe the interventions or strategies being compared, and state why they were chosen.
Time horizon	8	State the time horizon(s) over which costs and consequences are being evaluated, and say why appropriate.

(Continued)

Table 7.4 (Continued)   CHEERS Checklist Lists Items to Include When Reporting Economic Evaluations of Health

Section/Item	Item No.	Recommendation
Discount rate	9	Report the choice of discount rate(s) used for costs and outcomes and say why appropriate.
Choice of health outcomes	10	Describe what outcomes were used as the measure(s) of benefit in the evaluation and their relevance for the type of analysis performed.
Measurement of effectiveness	11a	Single study–based estimates: Describe fully the design features of the single effectiveness study and why the single study was a sufficient source of clinical effectiveness data.
	11b	Synthesis-based estimates: Describe fully the methods used to identify included studies and synthesize clinical effectiveness data.
Measurement and valuation of preference-based outcomes	12	If applicable, describe the population and methods used to elicit preferences for outcomes.
Estimating resources and costs	13a	Single study–based economic evaluation: Describe approaches used to estimate resource use associated with the alternative interventions. Describe primary or secondary research methods for valuing each resource item in terms of its unit cost. Describe any adjustments made to approximate to opportunity costs.

(*Continued*)

Table 7.4 (Continued)   CHEERS Checklist Lists Items to Include When Reporting Economic Evaluations of Health

Section/Item	Item No.	Recommendation
	13b	Model-based economic evaluation: Describe approaches and data sources used to estimate resource use associated with model health states. Describe primary or secondary research methods for valuing each resource item in terms of its unit cost. Describe any adjustments made to approximate opportunity costs.
Currency, price, date, and conversion	14	Report the dates of the estimated resource quantities and unit costs. Describe methods for adjusting estimated unit costs to the year of reported costs if necessary. Describe methods for converting costs into a common currency base and the exchange rate.
Choice of model	15	Describe and give reasons for the specific type of decision-analytical model used. Providing a figure to show model structure is strongly recommended.
Assumptions	16	Describe all structural or other assumptions underpinning the decision-analytical model.
Analytical methods	17	Describe all analytical methods supporting the evaluation. This could include methods for dealing with skewed, missing, or censored data; extrapolation methods; methods for pooling data; approaches to validate or make adjustments (such as half-cycle corrections) to a model; and methods for handling population heterogeneity and uncertainty.

(Continued)

Table 7.4 (Continued)   CHEERS Checklist Lists Items to Include When Reporting Economic Evaluations of Health

Section/Item	Item No.	Recommendation
Results		
Study parameters	18	Report the values, ranges, references, and, if used, probability distributions for all parameters. Report reasons or sources for distributions used to represent uncertainty where appropriate. Providing a table to show the input values is strongly recommended.
Incremental costs and outcomes	19	For each intervention, report mean values for the main categories of estimated costs and outcomes of interest, as well as mean differences between the comparator groups. If applicable, report incremental cost-effectiveness ratios.
Characterizing uncertainty	20a	Single study–based economic evaluation: Describe the effects of sampling uncertainty for the estimated incremental cost and incremental effectiveness parameters, together with the impact of methodological assumptions (such as discount rate and study perspective).
	20b	Model-based economic evaluation: Describe the effects on the results of uncertainty for all input parameters, and uncertainty related to the structure of the model and assumptions.

(Continued)

Table 7.4 (Continued)   CHEERS Checklist Lists Items to Include When Reporting Economic Evaluations of Health

Section/Item	Item No.	Recommendation
Characterizing heterogeneity	21	If applicable, report differences in costs, outcomes, or cost-effectiveness that can be explained by variations between subgroups of patients with different baseline characteristics or other observed variability in effects that are not reducible by more information.
Discussion		
Study findings, limitations, generalizability, and current knowledge	22	Summarize key study findings and describe how they support the conclusions reached. Discuss limitations and the generalizability of the findings and how the findings fit with current knowledge.
Other		
Source of funding	23	Describe how the study was funded and the role of the funder in the identification, design, conduct, and reporting of the analysis. Describe other nonmonetary sources of support.
Conflicts of interest	24	Describe any potential for conflict of interest of study contributors in accordance with journal policy. In the absence of a journal policy, we recommend authors comply with the International Committee of Medical Journal Editors recommendations.

Source: Based on the Equator network (http://www.equator-network. org/reporting-guidelines/cheers/).

The value of HIT cannot be expressed solely in economic terms. In reality, decision makers need to be able to justify investment, which makes economic evaluations necessary.[2]

Suggested Reading

Bassi J, Lau F. Measuring value for money: A scoping review on economic evaluation of health information systems. *J Am Med Inform Assoc*. 2014;20(4):792–801. PMID: 23416247. Review of summarized publications on HIT economic evaluation in terms of the types of economic analysis, covered areas, and others.

Drummond MF, Sculpher MJ, Torrance GW, O'Brien BJ, Stoddart GL. *Methods for the Economic Evaluation of Health Care Programmes*. 3rd edn. Oxford: Oxford University Press, 2005. ISBN: 0198529457.

ROI research in healthcare: The value factor in returns on health IT investments. http://apps.himss.org/transformation/docs/ResearchReport1.pdf.

Swensen SJ, Dilling JA, McCarty PM, Bolton JW, Harper CM. The business case for health-care quality improvement. *J Patient Saf*. 2013;9(1):44–52. PMID: 23429226.

Tan-Torres Edejer T, Baltussen R, Adam T. et al. (eds) *Making Choices in Health: WHO Guide to Cost-Effectiveness Analysis*. http://www.who.int/choice/publications/p_2003_generalised_cea.pdf.

U.S. National Library of Medicine. Health economics information resources: A self-study course. https://www.nlm.nih.gov/nichsr/edu/healthecon/index.html.

Wang T, Biedermann S. Running the numbers on an EHR: Applying cost-benefit analysis in EHR adoption. http://bok.ahima.org/doc?oid=101607.

References

1. McLaughlin N, Ong MK, Tabbush V, Hagigi F, Martin NA. Contemporary health care economics: An overview. *Neurosurg Focus*. 2014;37(5):E2. doi:10.3171/2014.8.FOCUS14455. PMID: 25363430.

2. Bassi J, Lau F. Measuring value for money: A scoping review on economic evaluation of health information systems. *J Am Med Inform Assoc*. 2013;20(4):792–801. doi:10.1136/amia-jnl-2012-001422. PMID: 23416247.

3. Choi JS, Lee WB, Rhee P-L. Cost-benefit analysis of electronic medical record system at a tertiary care hospital. *Healthc Inform Res*. 2013;19(3):205–214. doi:10.4258/hir.2013.19.3.205. PMID: 24175119.

4. Mauskopf JA, Paul JE, Grant DM, Stergachis A. The role of cost-consequence analysis in healthcare decision-making. *Pharmacoeconomics*. 1998;13(3):277–288. http://www.ncbi.nlm.nih.gov/pubmed/10178653.PMID: 10178653.

5. Raftery J. Methodological limitations of cost-effectiveness analysis in health care: Implications for decision making and service provision. *J Eval Clin Pract*. 1999;5(4): 361–366. http://www.ncbi.nlm.nih.gov/pubmed/10579700. PMID: 10579700.

6. Weintraub WS, Cohen DJ. The limits of cost-effectiveness analysis. *Circ Cardiovasc Qual Outcomes*. 2009;2(1):55–58. doi:10.1161/circoutcomes.108.812321. PMID: 20031813.

7. Detsky AS, Naglie IG. A clinician's guide to cost-effectiveness analysis. *Ann Intern Med*. 1990;113(2):147–154. http://www.ncbi.nlm.nih.gov/pubmed/2113784. PMID: 2113784.

8. Wu RC, Laporte A, Ungar WJ. Cost-effectiveness of an electronic medication ordering and administration system in reducing adverse drug events. *J Eval Clin Pract*. 2007;13(3):440–448. doi:10.1111/j.1365-2753.2006.00738.x. PMID: 17518812.

9. Karnon J, McIntosh A, Dean J, et al. Modelling the expected net benefits of interventions to reduce the burden of medication errors. *J Health Serv Res Policy*. 2008;13(2):85–91. doi:10.1258/jhsrp.2007.007011. PMID: 18416913.

10. Buysse H, De Moor G, Van Maele G, Baert E, Thienpont G, Temmerman M. Cost-effectiveness of telemonitoring for high-risk pregnant women. *Int J Med Inform*. 2008;77(7):470–476. doi:10.1016/j.ijmedinf.2007.08.009. PMID: 17923433.

11. Driessen J, Cioffi M, Alide N, et al. Modeling return on investment for an electronic medical record system in Lilongwe, Malawi. *J Am Med Inform Assoc*. 20(4):743–748. doi:10.1136/amiajnl-2012-001242. PMID: 23144335.

12. Husereau D, Drummond M, Petrou S, et al. Consolidated Health Economic Evaluation Reporting Standards (CHEERS) statement. *Int J Technol Assess Health Care*. 2013;29(2):117–122. doi:10.1017/S0266462313000160. PMID: 23587340.

Chapter 8

Efficacy and Effectiveness Evaluation

As we indicated in Chapter 1, the difference between the goals of official certification and regulatory compliance evaluation for the purpose of the current book is to set up an agenda for a clinically meaningful evaluation to prove (or disprove) that a particular information technology (IT) has an impact on clinically important outcomes, which are grouped into three broader categories (more details in Chapter 3)[1]:

- Better health (clinical outcome measurements). Examples are rate of intensive care unit (ICU)-acquired complications, discharge home, hospital mortality, and ICU and hospital readmission.
- Better care (clinical process measurements). Examples are adherence to and appropriateness of processes of care and provider satisfaction.
- Lower cost (financial impact measurements). Examples are resource utilization and severity-adjusted length of ICU and hospital stay and cost. A financial evaluation using

specific methods is described in Chapter 7. However, information on that part of the evaluation could be obtained during clinical effectiveness studies.

At this point, we need to define the terms *efficacy* and *effectiveness*. In fact, *effectiveness* is widely used in usability studies but with a meaning different from that used in the world of epidemiological research.

Efficacy: Measures what it is supposed to measure under an *ideal* condition. Efficacy is the measurement of the ability of the intervention to have effects without necessarily being relevant to patients. Such studies are performed in a highly controlled environment with highly compliant participants. In clinical research, such studies are called *explanatory trials* or Phase I or II of clinical trials. In healthcare information technology (HIT or health IT) evaluation, we can call them "lab studies."

Effectiveness: Measures what it is supposed to measure under an *average* condition. Effectiveness is the ability of an intervention to have effects on patients in normal clinical conditions. In clinical research, such studies are called *pragmatic trials* or Phase III or IV of clinical trials. In HIT evaluation, these studies include "live" implementation.

The relationships of these concepts are summarized in Figure 8.1.

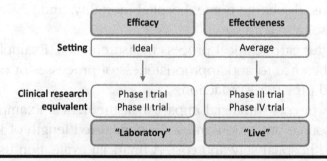

Figure 8.1 Efficacy and effectiveness in HIT evaluation.

A clinically oriented HIT evaluation should start with broad questions:

1. Does the technology function as intended?
2. Does the technology have the potential to be beneficial in the real world?

To answer these two questions, we should appropriately design studies that should start by defining the following:

1. Stakeholders. The results of the two types of studies described in the current chapter are a subject of concern for all stakeholders—patients, users/clinicians, developers, administrators, and regulatory agencies.
2. Study objective/aim. Broad studies could aim for function, effect, or impact.
3. Study subjects. Usually, users of technology or patients.
4. Version of technology. Prototype at any stage or release. Because a study could be timely or costly and nonrevertible, this should be carefully considered.
5. Study setting. Depends on the study aims, which could be a laboratory or a real-life setting.
6. Study tasks. Could be divided into two categories: simulated and real.

A simple framework for developing your own guide for the outcome assessment of HIT efficacy and efficiency could be outlined as follows:

1. What (outcomes of HIT implementation)
2. Where (evaluation setting—lab vs. live)
3. How (evaluation methods)
4. When (evaluation timing)

8.1 Clinically Oriented Outcomes of Interest (What)

When we evaluate technology, we should look for some improvement on what is currently available. Many see improvement of patient outcome as a synonym of mortality. However, because clinical medicine is so complex, showing that health IT improves outcomes in terms of mortality may be impossible.

Instead, the target of an outcome evaluation should be more granular and specific.

It could be divided into different levels representing different health concepts:

1. Biological, genetic, and molecular factors. HIT has no ability to influence those factors.
2. Symptoms. Include physical, psychological, emotional, and psychological symptoms.
3. Functional status. Physical and psychological functioning and social role.
4. General health perception. This is included in the subjective rating of the general health.
5. Overall quality of life. Integrative, adjusted to expectation, objective, and subjective measurements.

A number of factors have an impact on the success of HIT and could be described as objective measurement. All of them could be evaluated during system development and implementation:

1. System quality. A poorly constructed, unreliable system has little chance of being clinically successful moving forward.
2. Information quality. A well-known concept is "garbage in, garbage out." The best system will be unsuccessful if the

data used have gaps or are mislabeling or unreliable from a technical standpoint.

3. User satisfaction. An important factor that predefines further success. With high expectations, a new system should be pleasant to use.
4. Adoption. The best system will show no impact if it is not used. The first three factors and administrative/implementation efforts are key to influencing usage.
5. Acceptability. The perception of users and stakeholders that the system is doing an important practice.
6. Feasibility. The measurement that a particular system could be carried out during implementation.
7. Sustainability. The measurement that a particular system could be carried out after implementation.
8. Implementation cost. Monetary cost pertinent to implementation and related services excluding long-term support.
9. Individual impact. This is the actual clinical outcome, and it is most important from the perspective of clinical success.
10. Organizational impact. For the healthcare organization, success will most likely be measured with different monetary and nonmonetary costs.

In practice settings, two frequently used outcomes that are associated with individual and organizational impacts are clinical and financial outcomes. However, user satisfaction is increasingly becoming an important metric. A number of tools and measurements are available for use:

1. Questionnaire for User Interaction Satisfaction (QUIS). Targeting general computer system users.[2]
2. Perceived Usefulness Scale (PEU). Targeting clinicians.[3]
3. Questionnaire on Computer Systems and Decision Making. Targeting IT managers.[4]

All systems use Likert scale versions in questionnaires.

A more specific area of concern for the HIT impact would be organized around the following domains:

- Better diagnosis
- Better therapy
- Better communication (clinician to clinician or clinician to patient)
- Better knowledge management (clinician or patient)
- Less time spent on the care process (clinicians or patients)
- Less expensive care
- Safer care

In the evaluation process, what has higher priority and importance should be prioritized.

8.2 Settings for Evaluation (Where)

The eventual goal of any evaluation is to show the impact of technology on the real-world problem in a typical situation. However, in many situations this may be impossible to do. Thus, evaluation in the laboratory could be used as an approximation. The main advantage of a lab study is its controlled environment, which is safe for patients. Another advantage that a laboratory allows is modifying a test situation to a wider extent. Its disadvantage is that oftentimes investigators experience a situation wherein tested clinicians perform differently than they do in a typical clinical situation.

Live experiments show a real-world performance; however, they are prone to biases and confounders. Isolating informatics intervention from other initiatives is difficult. On the positive side, a tested IT solution shows a very crude performance. Live experiments can be performed in most clinical settings as technologies are involved at different stages of the care process. A clinical setting should be chosen based on a tested technology. A couple of levels of evaluation could be structured as follows:

1. Nationwide (diverse healthcare organizations)
2. Healthcare delivery system (multiple-facilities organization)
3. Single healthcare organization (hospital, clinic)
4. Location-based structured part (ward, ICU, operating room [OR])
5. Clinical care team (service, department)
6. Individual clinician (medical doctor [MD], registered nurse [RN])
7. Individual patient or case
8. Information as resource (electronic medical record [EMR], picture archiving and communication system [PACS])
9. Specific component of information (laboratory results)

Using this simple structure at the planning stage, the investigator could target a specific level for HIT evaluation.

8.3 Evaluation Methods (How)

The correct methodology plays a vital role in the end results. In Chapters 2 and 3, we discussed the design of evaluation studies. To recap, the best study design depends on multiple factors. A simple guide to choosing the best type of study in a live environment is shown in Table 8.1.

A laboratory setting has its own limitations, including observational bias, the Hawthorn effect, and the limited number of tasks that can be tested. A tested task can target four core cognitive tasks: memorizing/recalling, computation, decision support, and collaboration. Based on those tasks, a specific method should be chosen.

Without implementation research (effectiveness studies), we can only hope that the implemented HIT will work out well

Table 8.1 Choosing a Study Type for HIT Evaluation

	Simple Before-After	*Controlled Before-After*	*Randomized Trial*
Typical use of study results	Local decisions	Regional decisions	National policy decisions
Study scope	Identifying the effect	Describing the effect	Determining the cause and size of the effect
Detectable change	Large	Medium	Small
Chance of bias	Very high	Medium	Low if well designed
Setting	Single organization	Single or consortium of two to five organizations	Any; more is better
Cost of study	Low	Low or medium	Medium or usually high

Source: Adapted from Wyatt, J.C. and Wyatt, S.M., *Int J Med Inform,* 69(2–3), 251–259, 2003.

in terms of outcome impact. Despite the importance of effectiveness research, it has been neglected for two reasons: first, a lack of understanding of what it is and what it could offer exists, and second, a lack of budget for such studies presents a problem.

However, implementation research could be embedded in a classical PDSA (plan, do, study, act) cycle, and results could greatly enhance the end goal. Research can be used at any stage of the process.

These principles could be used in HIT development and evaluation. As Step 1 is mostly important for the design phase,

Steps 2 and 3 would be a perfect fit for the initial small pilot studies in a laboratory setting (efficiency study) and live implementation.

8.4 Evaluation Timing (When)

In the context of HIT evaluation, it could be organized around a specific task of a component of the clinical workflow. Identifying clinical processes and understanding how technology can improve care should be clearly defined. This requires testing a specific process of care target. Planning this investigation should clearly define what stage in the care process would be studied. This predefines a specific time frame for observation.

Figure 8.2 shows the major stages in the care process and the tasks performed by different clinical and office personnel during a typical office visit.

A final version of the technology should have a clear description of the intended workflow to be addressed in the evaluation study.

8.5 Example of HIT Evaluation Studies

Scientific journal articles could serve as great examples of a methodology and analysis plan. The following sections are examples of three types of studies often used in HIT evaluation: simple before-after, survey analysis, and validation against a gold standard.

Example of a Survey Analysis Study

Human knowledge is valuable information that could be used in initial requirement gathering and user experience (satisfaction/usability) evaluation. The problem is how to capture such information that could be representative and valid.

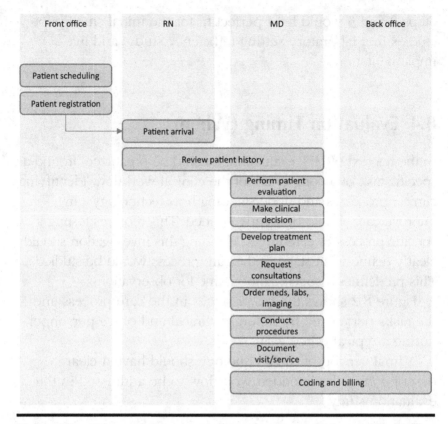

Figure 8.2 Schematic representation of major tasks in a typical office visit (RN: register nurse, MD: medical doctor).

A well-designed validated survey with a high response rate would be ideal from a scientific point of view. However, often more practical would be a modified Delphi survey. The article "Information Needs for the OR and PACU Electronic Medical Record"[5] published in the *Applied Clinical Informatics* journal aimed to understand the intraoperative and postanesthesia clinical information needs of anesthesia providers. This knowledge could be used for designing the future generation of EMR. From a methodological standpoint, it was a web-based survey at an academic medical center. A survey was distributed to all anesthesia providers: attending physicians (AP), certified registered nurse anesthetists (CRNA), anesthesia residents and fellows (physicians in training [PT]), and student registered nurse anesthetists (SRNA). A survey development process included an expert panel who identified important EMR data elements. Based on this information, a survey using a seven-point Likert scale was created. The free survey distribution mechanism LimeSurvey (www.limesurvey.org) package was used. This web-based stand-alone tool allowed the use of a survey inside a firewall. An invitation to participate was sent via e-mail. Analysis included the Kruskal–Wallis test (ANOVA), the Tukey–Kramer test, and the Bland–Altman plot analysis. The response rate averaged 26% with a range of groups of providers from 10% to 36%. The lessons learned from this article include the necessity to engage leadership to achieve an acceptable response rate, build a clinically meaningful survey, and inform clinicians about the future use of information received as a result of the study. The limitation of the described study is that it is a single institution experience that can be different in other healthcare organizations.

Example of a Gold Standard Validation Study

A new diagnostic method developed a (not only laboratory but also technological) confirmation of diagnostic performance, which is required to show that the system performs adequately. This absolutely "must be" tested for the clinical validation of new alerts of surveillance systems. The evaluation of such systems is based on a well-established methodology that has been long used in laboratory medicine. An example of a diagnostic performance study for the evaluation of an alert system is the article "Customized Reference Ranges for Laboratory Values Decrease False Positive Alerts in Intensive Care Unit Patients,"[6] which had the objective of comparing sensitivity, specificity, and predictive values for abnormal laboratory value indicators between novel and traditional EMR systems. Two board-certified critical care physicians independently evaluated patients' problem lists and marked the test results about which they would like to be alerted given the patients' diagnoses. Disagreements were resolved by a third board-certified critical care physician making the final decision. This was used as a "gold standard." After that, both system alerts were compared with the "gold standard." The main results were reported as sensitivity, specificity, and positive and negative predictive values (PPV, NPV). Additional reported statistics were the demographic characteristics of the cohort and interobserver agreement. This type of study gives a clear answer to which alert is better and how good it is compared with the best possible "gold standard." The major limitation of this type of study is the quality of the "gold standard." If the objective measurement or standard is not available, two reviewers should contribute to the assessment. All discrepancies should be resolved by consensus or a third "super-reviewer."

Example of a Before-After Study

A before-after study in HIT evaluation looks like a natural step to show the value of a new technology. However, an uncontrolled design is prone to significant bias that could affect the results in a way that could make them completely inaccurate.

When investigators design this type of study in the planning phase, they should pay attention to details and, as much as possible, eliminate the influence of other factors or describe them in the limitation part of the report, including the estimated size effect.

As an example, we use a study that utilizes an EMR to improve the quality of urban pediatric primary care.[7] The objective of this study was to evaluate the quality of pediatric primary care in an urban pediatric primary care center before and after the introduction of EMR. The intervention was the implementation of a pediatric EMR. The study tested three hypotheses: (1) a comprehensive EMR could be designed and successfully implemented in a busy urban primary care center; (2) the quality of the documentation of a comprehensive set of primary care measures would improve after the introduction of the EMR; and (3) specific outcomes such as immunization status would improve with the use of the EMR. The study assistant and the participating clinicians were blinded to the study goals. The statistical methodology included a chi-square test for the comparison of categorical data and the *t*-test for a comparison of continuous data. A 20-question satisfaction survey was used a year later after successful implementation. The reported statistics included relative risk (RR) with 95% confidence interval (CI). The discussion part included comments on the limitations of the before-after study. It is important to mention that the supplementary satisfaction survey gained additional information about the potential benefits of the system, the numerical effect was biased overall, and the success of the system could be estimated.

8.6 Security Evaluation

No other HIT questions have garnered more attention in recent years than information security. The up-to-date statistics show that in 2015, data breaches in the United States totaling more than 112 million health records affected approximately 34.7% of the population. Nine out of the 10 biggest breaches were labeled as a "hacking/IT incident." As no specific recommendations exist for the evaluation of the HIT technology with regard to security for the purpose of general performance evaluation, we decided to provide basic information as a "starter kit." From a regulatory point of view, the Health Insurance Portability and Accountability Act of 1996 (HIPPA) established security and privacy regulations. The HIPAA security rule (45 CFR Part 160 and Subparts A and C of Part 164) requires covered entities to perform a periodic technical and nontechnical security evaluation. The HIPPA requires that standard transaction formats be used for electronic data interchange (EDI) of healthcare data. An EHR with appropriate backup procedures provides safety that could never be achieved with paper charts. The HIPAA privacy rule can be found on 45 CFR Part 160 and Part 164, Subparts A and E.

In general, three different safeguards are required for the security of protected health information (PHI) when using HIT:

1. Administrative safeguards. Administrative actions, policies, and procedures to protect the security, privacy, and confidentiality of patients' PHI.
2. Physical safeguards. Physical measures, policies, and procedures to protect workstations, IT infrastructure and equipment, and related facilities from natural hazards and unauthorized access.
3. Technical safeguards. Technology that protects electronic health information and controls access to it.

Administrative and physical safeguards are outside the focus of electronic system development and should be addressed appropriately. Technical safeguards should be built into and addressed by the HIT system in the best-case scenario at the design phase. The following elements of technical safeguards should be addressed:

■ Access control. Allowing access only to persons or software programs that have appropriate access rights to particular data elements or PHI.
■ Audit control. Recording and examining the activity in HIT systems that contain or use PHI.
■ Integrity. Protecting PHI from improper alteration or destruction.
■ Person authentication. Verifying that a person seeking access to PHI is who or what he or she claims to be (proof of identity).
■ Transmission security. Guarding against unauthorized access to PHI that is being transmitted over an electronic communications network.

HealthIT.gov provides security risk assessment information (https://www.healthit.gov/providers-professionals/security-risk-assessment). This information is for informational purposes only. The Office of the National Coordinator of Health Information Technology (ONC), in collaboration with the U.S. Department of Health and Human Services (HHS) Office for Civil Rights (OCR) and the HHS Office of the General Counsel (OGC), developed a security risk assessment tool (SRA tool). The SRA tool is downloadable, but its use is neither required by nor guarantees compliance with federal, state, or local laws.

At this point, professional services and trusted commercial companies recommend security evaluation.

Suggested Reading

45 CFR Parts 160 and 164 Modifications to the HIPAA Privacy, Security, Enforcement, and Breach Notification Rules Under the Health Information Technology for Economic and Clinical Health Act and the Genetic Information Nondiscrimination Act. https://www.gpo.gov/fdsys/pkg/FR-2013-01-25/pdf/2013-01073.pdf.

Altman DG, Royston P. What do we mean by validating a prognostic model? *Stat Med*. 2000;19(4):453–473. PMID: 10694730.

Kozma CM, Reeder CE, Schultz RM. Economic, clinical, and humanistic outcomes: A planning model for pharmacoeconomic research. *Clin Ther*. 1993;15(6):1121–1132. The Economic, Clinical, and Humanistic Outcomes (ECHO) model depicts the value of a pharmaceutical product or service as a combination of traditional clinical-based outcomes with more contemporary measures of economic efficiency and quality.

Reassessing your security practices in a health IT environment: A guide for small health care practices. http://s3.amazonaws.com/rdcms-himss/files/production/public/HIMSSorg/Content/files/Code%20165%20HHS%20Reassessing%20Security%20Practices%20in%20a%20Health%20IT%20Environment.pdf.

Scales DC, Laupacis A. Health technology assessment in critical care. *Intensive Care Med*. 2007;33(12):2183–2191. PMID: 17952404.

Summary of the HIPPA privacy rule. https://www.hhs.gov/sites/
default/files/privacysummary.pdf.

References

1. Roundtable on Value & Science-Driven Health Care; Institute
   of Medicine. *Core Measurement Needs for Better Care, Better
   Health, and Lower Costs: Counting What Counts: Workshop
   Summary*. Washington, DC: National Academies Press; 2013
   Aug 30. 1, Introd.
2. Chin JP, Diehl VA, Norman KL. Development of an instrument
   measuring user satisfaction of the human–computer interface. In *ACM CHI'88 Proceedings, Proceedings of the SIGCHI
   Conference on Human Factors in Computing Systems* (pp.
   213–218). New York: ACM, 1988.
3. Davis, F. Perceived usefulness, perceived ease of use, and
   user acceptance of information technology. *MIS Quarterly*.
   1989;13(3):319–340.
4. Hatcher M. Information systems' approaches and designs and
   facility information: Survey of acute care hospitals in the United
   States. *J Med Syst*. 1998;22(6):389–396.
5. Herasevich V, Ellsworth MA, Hebl JR, Brown MJ, Pickering BW.
   Information needs for the OR and PACU electronic medical
   record. *Appl Clin Inform*. 2014;5(3):630–641.
6. Kilickaya O, Schmickl C, Ahmed A, et al. Customized reference
   ranges for laboratory values decrease false positive alerts in
   intensive care unit patients. *PLoS One*. 2014;9(9):e107930.
7. Adams WG, Mann AM, Bauchner H. Use of an electronic medical record improves the quality of urban pediatric primary
   care. *Pediatrics*. 2003;111(3):626–632. http://www.ncbi.nlm.nih.
   gov/pubmed/12612247.

Chapter 9

Usability Evaluation

For many, usability is one of the main factors that determine preference for a product. This is especially true in the software world. If two software products have equal functionalities to do tasks, would you prefer one with better or poorer usability? In the early years, usability was usually a component "without budget to develop." If software developers had freedom to interpret specifications and had sense and interest in usability, software products would have more chances to be "human friendly."

One should understand that developers are still limited by frameworks and programming languages that are used to develop visual interfaces. They have evolved over time; however, this situation continues to be the case in the modern world.

Usability is defined as the effectiveness, efficiency, and satisfaction with which specific users can achieve a specific set of tasks in a particular environment. This definition implies that usability can vary by context (i.e., user, task, or environment) or by measurement modality (i.e., effectiveness, efficiency, or satisfaction). Dr. Ronald Schoeffel defines *usability* as the quality of a product to operate easily.

When designing usability evaluation tools, one should identify the context and appropriately weigh the value of each measurement for the task at hand. For example, efficiency may be the most important consideration for the secretary checking a patient in the oncology clinic, but effectiveness may be more significant to the patient and provider when selecting an appropriate chemotherapy treatment option for a newly diagnosed cancer.

Let us look more closely at the measurement modalities—efficiency, effectiveness, and satisfaction.

9.1 Evaluation of Efficiency

Efficiency is generally considered the speed with which users can complete their tasks. Some key considerations for this metric include:

1. Identification of key processes critical for the successful completion of a task
2. Identification of key resources required to complete a task
3. Agreement on targets for acceptable completion times of these tasks

While efficiency is more important in some settings than in others, some measure of time-to-task completion should be included in any study of usability.

A measure of efficiency is usually included in any usability evaluation. It provides some insight into the potential technology that disrupts workflow in a detrimental fashion. Efficiency can be measured objectively as the

1. Time to accomplish a task (average, standard deviation)
2. Number (average, standard deviation) of clicks and keyboard/input device interactions to accomplish a task

9.2 Effectiveness and Evaluation of Errors

Effectiveness is defined as the accuracy and completeness with which users perform a task. This measure considers how easy it is for users to make and/or correct errors as they perform a given task. Since user errors can compromise a patient's safety, this component of usability is often weighted more heavily than others in the healthcare setting. One key limitation of this measure is how it tends to focus on individual tasks or task components without placing them in the context of the other competing tasks. To counterbalance this, a measure of perceived individual and team performance is considered. In particular, we have found it very useful to include measures of individual and team safety in this section. These are excellent indicators of the impact of technology on the broader function of the team. They can identify unexpected degradation of critical team functions such as communication and provide big-picture insights that can be missed.

Imagine evaluating a system for a computerized drug order entry that has been designed to eliminate errors in prescribing. It will likely score very well on accuracy and completeness of drug order entry. Without a measure of the impact on the broader team performance, however, you would miss the fact that the system is so cumbersome that it consumes team resources and impairs their ability to function in other areas.

Another key limitation in this measure is the tendency to focus on tasks that are easily defined and therefore scored as "completed accurately without error." Medical tasks, however, often take the form of clinical diagnosis and treatment decisions. Decision-making errors can be difficult to measure and are often not included under the realm of usability. This is an important oversight as diagnostic error and delay are thought to occur in 10%–20% of all clinician–patient encounters. Testing the claim that a technology enhances rather than impairs this important task is one of the greatest challenges encountered in the evaluation process.

The broader model for the analysis and understanding of the use-related risks of electronic health record (EHR) systems contains the following four components:

1. *Use error root causes*: These are aspects of the user interface design that induce use errors when interacting with the system.
2. *Risk parameters*: These are attributes regarding particular use errors (i.e., their severity, frequency, ability to be detected, and complexity).
3. *Evaluative indicators*: These are indications that users are having problems with the system, and are identified through direct observations of the system in use in situ through interviews or user surveys.
4. *Adverse events*: These are descriptions of the use error outcome and the standard classification of patient harm.

As previously noted, the evaluation of a technology's propensity to promote or suppress error is critical if we are not to cause widespread harm to patients. A use-related risk assessment methodology can be used to investigate aspects of the user experience that may contribute to error. We will discuss examples of this measure in the case studies presented in Chapter 10.

9.3 Evaluating Consistency of Experience (User Satisfaction)

User satisfaction is usually the first thing that people think in relation to "usability." Satisfaction in the context of usability refers to the subjective satisfaction a user may have with a process or outcome. Satisfaction is highly subjective, but routine questionnaires can provide a good insight into users' problems or issues with a system.

User satisfaction is one of the most underrated measurement modalities in healthcare. Generally, healthcare workers are a highly motivated and skilled workforce. They have a real sense of ownership and give excellent feedback when asked. All other things being equal, a product with high user satisfaction scores will almost certainly benefit patients the most. A closely related key component to consider in this metric is "intention to use." More on this topic can be found in the references and case studies in Chapter 10.

Efficiency, effectiveness, and satisfaction cannot be measured in isolation. All three components must be evaluated and balanced based on your practice's goals and priorities. Overemphasizing one component can lead to unexpected clinical outcomes when systems are deployed into widespread use. This is discussed again when we review some examples from our practice.

A number of documents and standards exist and are available for use. The comprehensive ISO 9241 is a multipart document covering the ergonomics of human–system interaction. ISO 20282-1:2006 is another document titled "Ease of Operation of Everyday Products—Part 1: Design Requirements for Context of Use and User Characteristics" that could be applied in the healthcare setting.

A key determinant of usability is the consistency of the user experience. Learning a new workflow or functional layout is disruptive to the end user, promotes error, reduces effectiveness and efficiency, and results in a poor user experience. Consistency is a product of good design and is measured using a subjective rating scale for the subdimensions of

1. Optimal placement of design elements (e.g., *cancel* buttons/controls)
2. Consistent labeling of design elements (e.g., a dialog box has the same label as the button that was pressed to open it)
3. Consistent use of keyboard shortcuts (e.g., Ctrl+C for copy)
4. Appropriate color coding of information (e.g., red for errors, yellow for alerts and warnings)

Table 9.1 Usability Approaches Summarized

Input	Characteristics	Strengths	Limitations
Lab	Test scenario	Scientific rigor	Only identified problems
Point of use	Voluntary, observations	Broader perspective	Analytical methodology for generalizability
Data mining	"Behind the scenes"	Actual use, no burden to users	Content expertise, generalizability
Surveys	Voluntary, subjective	Scientific rigor	Limited problems
Reporting	Voluntary	Detailed	More effort, subjective

5. Appropriate font size and type
6. Appropriate and consistent use of measurement units (e.g., kilograms)

These can be captured using a number of different techniques; each presents advantages and disadvantages as seen in Table 9.1.

9.4 Electronic Medical Record Usability Principles

Usability is an art for many, but it has a science rationale behind it. Experts who work on the concept of usability have identified gaps that affect the adoption of modern electronic medical record (EMR) and clinical informatics tools. To overcome these barriers, the principles of EMR usability should be organized around specific characteristics. Sometimes, it is difficult or impossible to apply these principles to the system in production. Using principles on design and development stage will improve the final product quality. Principles formulated by Jakob Nielsen with Rolf Molich in the early 1990s could be translated to an EMR design as well. In an effort to address the previously outlined concerns, the Healthcare Information and Management Systems Society (HIMSS) has identified nine usability principles that are important to consider when designing and evaluating EMR systems. These are summarized as follows:

- *Simplicity*: Include only important and limited-to-tasks interface elements in the clean design. The interface should not contain irrelevant or rarely needed information.
- *Naturalness*: Computer interfaces should be intuitive, address practice needs, and mimic metaphors in everyday life.
- *Consistency*: Terminology used and part of interface appeal the same throughout the whole software.
- *Forgiveness and feedback*: A mistake-proof design provides informative feedback to users.
- *Effective use of language*: Use standard clinical terminology/language. Data entry forms should be clear and natural.
- *Efficient interactions*: Minimize steps to achieve the goal. Reduce scrolling and clicking.
- *Effective information presentation*: Colors should be meaningful and consistent. Font size must be adequate.
- *Preservation of context*: Minimize visual interruption. Recognition rather than recall. The user should not have to remember how to use the system. Minimize cognitive load.
- Information needed for a particular task or for decision making is grouped on a single screen rather than requiring the user to mentally integrate information from multiple screens in the system.

- Alerts presented to the user are concise and informative with clear actions and are appropriate in number.
- The application performs calculations automatically for the clinician so that he or she does not have to manually perform the calculations.

The HIMSS principles of usability are a welcome addition to the discussion on healthcare technology and an excellent starting point for questions and research ideas in this domain.

9.5 Usability and the EHR Evaluation Process

Since the EHR is part of our healthcare environment, it is important to take some time to discuss usability as it relates to the EHR.

A compromised EHR system usability can have a number of significant and negative implications in a clinical setting. Two key concerns for the healthcare information technology (HIT or health IT) community are

1. Promotion of user errors that potentially cause patient harm
2. Impact of poor usability on EHR adoption rates

Areas that are emerging as concerns include the impact of usability on

1. Clinician burnout
2. Patient satisfaction

In 2012, the National Institute of Standards and Technology (NIST) published the document "Technical Evaluation, Testing, and Validation of the Usability of Electronic Health Records."[1]

The document presented the rationale for the EMR usability protocol (EUP) and defined the procedures for design and human user performance testing and evaluation. The EUP is a three-step process (see Figure 9.1):

1. EHR application analysis
2. EHR user interface expert review
3. EHR user interface validation testing

The first step is key for the application development process. It describes basic functions and users' interaction with the application. In the NIST guideline, it is reflected in the HIT application analysis part. Task analysis targets the description of interactions with the application and user as well as the identification of critical tasks that can affect patient safety.

The second step includes developers, usability experts, and the clinical safety team. They compare the user interface design to establish design principles and standards to identify issues that can increase safety risks and are described in the HIT interface expert review.

The third step is a real-life user performance study on critical tasks before actual implementation. The study could include objective measurements such as time-to-task completion, number of errors, and number of clicks (interactions), and a subjective rating scale through surveys. In the NIST guideline, it is represented by "Step III—HIT validation testing."

A Note on Evaluating the Real-World Usability of HIT

Literature supporting whether a HIT performs as expected or claimed by the manufacturer is difficult to find. Task-oriented evaluation of technology in the real world or in simulated real-world settings offers compelling insights into the usability of a technology. There are, however, few clinical trials of

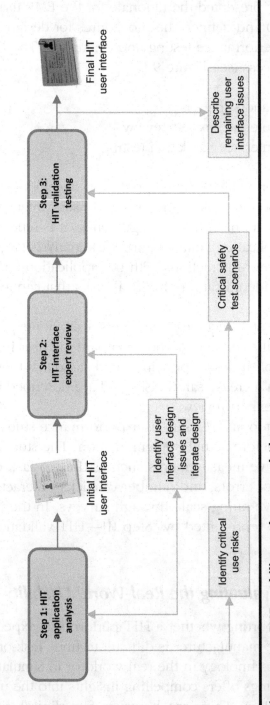

Figure 9.1 EHR usability study protocol (three-step process).

technology and almost no comparisons across manufacturers because clinical trials are difficult and expensive to perform.

A look at the pharmaceuticals industry offers some insight into the challenges of this approach. Should software manufacturers be expected to evaluate the usability of their products in a scientifically rigorous and reportable fashion? Should unsubstantiated claims about performance be tolerated? Do we consider HIT to be similar to the largely unregulated herbal supplement and alternative medicine space, or do we consider it to be more similar to the conventional pharmaceutical or medical device industry? As we move away from accounting and into an era when analytics and alerts are being pushed into clinical practice, we need to carefully consider these questions. Frameworks for the systematic evaluation of usability that would be adopted broadly will allow us to compare performance and claims with better reliability across manufacturers.

A number of attempts have been made to standardize user interfaces in clinical applications. Microsoft Health Common User Interface (MSCUI) was released in 2007. The aim of the MSCUI Design Guidance was to support the delivery of safe patient care by providing detailed guidance for the standardization of clinical application user interfaces (http://www.mscui.net/). However, no activities have been identified after 2010.

9.6 Usability Testing Approaches

A number of frameworks help evaluate the usability of technology in healthcare. However, no perfect scenario exists. Frameworks can be too generic or too specific and should be viewed as a starting point for evaluation rather than all-encompassing.

In Figure 9.2, the usability requirements are defined up front with stakeholders. One or several usability testing

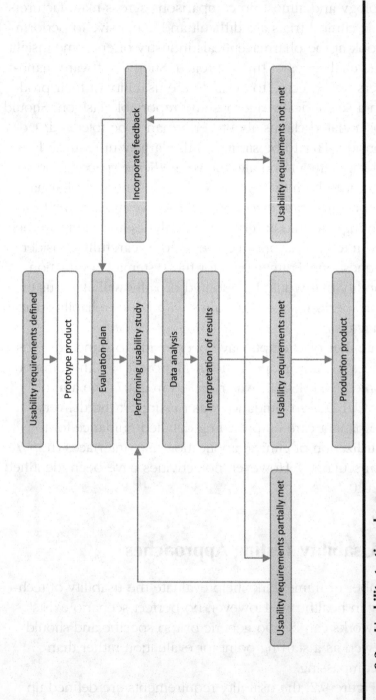

Figure 9.2   Usability testing phases.

methods are chosen to measure usability in the domains described earlier in this chapter. The evaluations are analyzed and interpreted before a judgment on usability requirements is made. Recommendations regarding the next steps (user interface design feedback) are given, and the cycle continues until usability requirements are met.

The academic community is also concerned with EHR usability. To facilitate the adoption and meaningful use of the EHR, an EHR-specific usability framework was developed. TURF (task, user, representation, and function) can be used to increase efficiency and productivity, ease of use and ease of learning, user retention, and satisfaction, and decrease human errors, development time and cost, and support and training cost. TURF targets four components that determine the usability of an EHR system.[2]

TURF's definition of usability is based on the ISO definition (ISO 9241-11 Ergonomic Requirements for Office Work with Visual Display Terminals [VDTs]—Part 11: Guidance on Usability) but differs from it in significant ways. *Useful*, *usable*, and *satisfying* are the three major dimensions of usability under TURF. Not only can usability be defined under a coherent, unified theoretical framework, but it can also be measured objectively and systematically.

9.7 Specific Usability Testing Methods

In the first half of this chapter, we outlined the need for the evaluation of usability and provided some principles to guide you in developing usability testing metrics for your practice. Now, we will outline a few specific methodological approaches that can be taken to evaluate user experience.

Cognitive Walk-Through

Cognitive walk-through involves one or a group of evaluators observing or interviewing a subject as he or she performs a task or tasks using a new technology. As the subject works, the observers evaluate understandability and ease of learning.

Key Features and Output

- *The user interface* is often presented in the form of a paper mock-up or a working prototype, but it can also be a fully developed interface.
- *The input* to the walk-through includes the user profile, especially the users' knowledge of the task domain, interface, and cases.
- *The evaluators* may include human factors (engineers, software developers, or people from marketing, documentation, etc.).
- *This technique* is best used in the design stage of development, but it can also be applied during the code, test, and deployment stages.

9.8 Procedure

Phase 1: Defining the Users of the System

Who will be the users of the system? This should include specific background experience or technical knowledge that could influence users as they attempt to deal with a new interface. The users' knowledge of both the task and the interface should be considered. An example user description is "Macintosh users who have worked with MacPaint."

Phase 2: Defining the Task(s) for the Walk-Through

What task(s) will be analyzed? In general, the system should be limited to a reasonable but representative collection of benchmark tasks. Task selection should be based on the results of marketing studies, needs analysis, concept testing, and requirements analyses.

Phase 3: Walking through the Actions and Critiquing Critical Information

What is the correct action sequence for each task? For each task, there must be a description of how the user is expected to view the task before learning the interface. There must also be a description of the sequence of actions that should accomplish the task with the current definition of the interface. Example actions are "press the Return key," and "move cursor to the **File** menu." It can also be a sequence of several simple actions that a typical user could execute as a block such as "Select Save from the **File** menu."

Phase 4: Summarization of the Walk-Through Results

How is the interface defined? The definition of the interface must describe the prompts preceding every action required to accomplish the tasks being analyzed as well as the reaction of the interface to each of these actions. If the interface has been implemented, all information would be available. Early in the development process, the evaluation can be performed with a paper description of the interface. For a paper description, the level of detail in defining the interface will depend on the expertise that the anticipated users have with existing systems.

Phase 5: Recommendations to Designers

The following four questions should be addressed:

- *Will the users try to achieve the right effect?* For example, their task is to print a document, but the first thing they have to do is select a printer. Will they know that they should select a printer?
- *Will the user notice that the correct action is available?* This relates to the visibility and understandability of actions in the interface.

- *Will the user associate the correct action with the effect to be achieved?* Users often use the "label-following" strategy, which leads them to select an action if its label matches the task description.
- *If the correct action is performed, will the user see that progress is being made toward the solution of the task?* This is to check the system feedback after the user executes the action.

A good reference for this methodology would be "The Cognitive Walkthrough Method: A Practitioner's Guide" by C. Wharton et al. in J. Nielsen and R. Mack's *Usability Inspection Methods*.

Keystroke-Level Model

The *keystroke-level model* (KLM) is a simplified version of GOMS (goals, operators, methods, and selection rules). It was proposed by Card and Moran (1980) as a method for predicting user performance.[3]

Key Features and Output

Using the KLM, execution time is estimated by listing the sequence operators and then summing the times of the individual operators. The KLM aggregates all perceptual and cognitive functions into a single value for an entire task using a heuristic. Also, the KLM does not employ selection rules.

The original KLM had the following six classes of operators:

- **K** for pressing a key
- **P** for pointing to a location on-screen with the mouse
- **H** for moving hands to home position on the keyboard
- **M** for mentally preparing to perform an action
- **R** for system response where the user waits for the system

For each operator, execution time is estimated. Additionally, a set of heuristic rules accounts for the mental preparation time.

The KLM was designed as a quick and easy design tool that could be used without deep knowledge of psychology. It saves time and resources on the prototype and tests users' recruitment.

Heuristic Evaluation

Heuristic evaluation is a usability inspection method in which the system is evaluated based on well-tested design principles such as the visibility of system status, user control and freedom, consistency and standards, flexibility, and efficiency of use. This methodology was developed by Jakob Nielsen[4] and modified by Zhang[5] (Nielsen, J., "Enhancing the Explanatory Power of Usability Heuristics," CHI'94 Conference Proceedings [1994]).

Key Features and Output

This method identifies usability problems based on established human factors principles. It will provide recommendations for design improvements. However, as the method relies on experts, the output will naturally emphasize interface functionality and design rather than the properties of the interaction between an actual user and the product.

- *Visibility of system status*: The system should always keep users informed about what is going on through appropriate feedback within a reasonable time.
- *Match between the system and the real world*: The system should speak the users' language with words, phrases, and concepts familiar to them rather than using system-oriented terms. Follow real-world conventions, making information appear in a natural and logical order.

- *User control and freedom*: Users often choose system functions by mistake and will need a clearly marked "emergency exit" to leave the unwanted state without having to go through an extended dialogue. Support undo and redo.
- *Consistency and standards*: Users should not have to wonder whether different words, situations, or actions mean the same thing. Follow platform conventions.
- *Error prevention*: Even better than good error messages is a careful design that prevents a problem from occurring in the first place. Either eliminate error-prone conditions or check for them and present users with a confirmation option before they commit to the action.
- *Recognition rather than recall*: Minimize the user's memory load by making objects, actions, and options visible. The user should not have to remember information from one part of the dialogue to another. Instructions for use of the system should be visible or easily retrievable whenever appropriate.
- *Flexibility and efficiency of use*: Accelerators—unseen by the novice user—may often speed up the interaction for the expert user such that the system can cater to both inexperienced and experienced users. Allow users to tailor frequent actions.
- *Aesthetic and minimalist design*: Dialogues should not contain irrelevant or rarely needed information. Every extra unit of information in a dialogue competes with the relevant units of information and diminishes their relative visibility.
- *Help users recognize, diagnose, and recover from errors*: Error messages should be expressed in plain language (no codes), precisely indicate the problem, and constructively suggest a solution.
- *Help and documentation*: Even though it is better if the system can be used without documentation, it may be necessary to provide help and documentation. Any such information should be easy to search, be focused on the

user's task, list concrete steps to be carried out, and not be too large.

Reporting

A list of identified problems that may be prioritized with regard to severity and/or safety criticality is produced.

In terms of summative output, the number of found problems, the estimated proportion of found problems compared with the theoretical total, and the estimated number of new problems expected to be found by including a specified number of new experts in the evaluation can also be provided.

The following are examples of heuristic evaluations lists:

ftp://ftp.cs.uregina.ca/pub/class/305/lab2/example-he.html: Heuristic Evaluation—A System Checklist by Deniese Pierotti, Xerox Corporation.
https://wiki.library.oregonstate.edu/confluence/download/ attachments/17959/Heuristic+Evaluation+Checklist. pdf: Heuristic Evaluation—A System Checklist, Usability Analysis & Design, WebCriteria, 2002.

System Usability Scale

The system usability scale (SUS) provides a "quick and dirty," reliable tool for measuring usability. It consists of a 10-item questionnaire with five response options for respondents—from *strongly agree* to *strongly disagree*. Originally created by John Brooke in 1986,[6] it allows you to evaluate a wide variety of products and services, including hardware, software, mobile devices, websites, and applications.

Benefits of Using an SUS

SUS has become an industry standard with references in over 1300 articles and publications. The noted benefits of using SUS include that it

1. Is a very easy scale to administer to participants
2. Can be used on small sample sizes with reliable results
3. Is valid—it can effectively differentiate between usable and unusable systems

Good information on SUS and the tool itself can be found in the following link: https://measuringu.com/sus/.

Table 9.2 summarizes the characteristics and features of the four usability methods widely applicable in health IT.

Table 9.2   Summary Characteristics of Common Usability Test Methods

	Cognitive Walk-Through	Keystroke-Level Model	Heuristic Evaluation	System Usability Scale (SUS)
Identifies errors affecting user performance	+			
Helps find serious problems	+			
Users with no previous training	+	−	+	
Used in the early stages of development	+			
Careful planning required	+			
Used at any stages of development		+		

(Continued)

Table 9.2 (Continued) Summary Characteristics of Common Usability Test Methods

	Cognitive Walk-Through	Keystroke-Level Model	Heuristic Evaluation	System Usability Scale (SUS)
Time estimation of user performance		+		
Used to compare alternative solutions		+		+
Economical		+	+	+
Can be used on noncomputer tasks		+		+
Quick to perform		+	+	+
Variance in results			+	
No identified positive functionality			+	
Preferred to be performed by expert evaluators			+	

9.9 Conclusions

Healthcare delivery requires that human and technological actors work in harmony to produce the desired health outcomes and avoid patient harm. Usability evaluation is important if we understand and anticipate the potential unintended consequences of technology such as patient harm, provider burnout, or reduced efficiency in our setting. As we move to an era of real-time clinical analytics and alerting, issues around usability must be systematically addressed. Independent evaluation of usability in real-world environments is essential if we are to enhance rather than impair the ability of health professionals to deliver high-quality care to our patients.

Suggested Reading

(NISTIR 7804) Technical evaluation, testing, and validation of the usability of electronic health records (2012). http://www.nist.gov/healthcare/usability/upload/EUP_WERB_Version_2_23_12-Final-2.pdf.

(NISTIR 7804-1) Technical evaluation, testing, and validation of the usability of electronic health records: Empirically based use cases for validating safety-enhanced usability and guidelines for standardization literature (2015). http://nvlpubs.nist.gov/nistpubs/ir/2015/NIST.IR.7804-1.pdf.

Electronic Health record usability: Interface design considerations. Prepared for AHRQ. http://healthit.ahrq.gov/sites/default/files/docs/citation/09-10-0091-2-EF.pdf.

HIMSS EHR Usability Task Force (2010). Selecting an EHR for your practice: Evaluating usability. http://www.himss.org/selecting-ehr-your-practice-evaluating-usability-himss.

Usability.gov is the leading resource for user experience (UX), best practices, and guidelines, serving practitioners and students in the government and private sectors. The site provides overviews of the user-centered design process and various UX disciplines. It also covers the related information on methodology and tools for making digital content more usable and useful. http://www.usability.gov/.

References

1. (NISTIR 7804) Technical evaluation, testing and validation of the usability of electronic health records. https://www.nist.gov/publications/nistir-7804-technical-evaluation-testing-and-validation-usability-electronic-health. 2012.

2. Zhang J, Walji MF. TURF: Toward a unified framework of EHR usability. *J Biomed Inform*. 2011;44(6):1056–1067. doi:10.1016/j.jbi.2011.08.005.
3. Card SK, Moran TP, Allen N. The keystroke-level model for user performance time with interactive systems. *Commun ACM*. 1980;23(7):396–410.
4. Nielsen J. Enhancing the explanatory power of usability heuristics. In: *Proceedings of the SIGCHI Conference on Human Factors in Computing Systems*. Vol. CHI '94. New York: ACM; 1994:152–158. doi:10.1145/191666.191729.
5. Zhang J, Johnson TR, Patel VL, Paige DL, Kubose T. Using usability heuristics to evaluate patient safety of medical devices. *J Biomed Inform*. 36(1–2):23–30. http://www.ncbi.nlm.nih.gov/pubmed/14552844.
6. Brooke J. SUS: A quick and dirty usability scale. *Usability Eval Ind*. 1996;189(194):4–7.

Chapter 10

Case Studies

The successful development and deployment of informatics tools for clinical practice is by necessity a multistep process. Tools that appear perfect in the development environment can surprise the developers by either failing in the clinical phase or by being utilized in ways they did not intend. This can lead to unintended consequences which are more often harmful than helpful. For this reason, developed tools must be carefully evaluated as they pass through the design, prototype, pilot, and full implementation phases in order to be considered safe for clinical practice. A post-surveillance phase is also recommended for tools that have the potential to directly impact on clinical decision making or patient care. In this chapter, we will present two examples of tools that have been developed and observed through these phases in clinical practice. The first case describes a technology that failed to deliver the expected impact and the second case is the story of an electronic tool that delivered the expected impact on practice.

10.1 Case Study 1: SWIFT Score

Rationale

Intensive care unit (ICU) readmissions are costly and associated with much worse outcomes for patients compared to those who are not readmitted. The clinical practice at our institution articulated a need to reduce readmission rates. At the time, our clinical research group had just developed and validated a clinical readmission risk factor calculator, the SWIFT score,[1] in precisely the patient population we were hoping to target in a quality improvement intervention to reduce readmission rates. The score was developed to provide some objective data to supplement a clinician's decision making regarding patient readiness for discharge.

SWIFT Score Development

The SWIFT score was developed using a development and testing database of patient data stored in the ICU DataMart.[2] The ICU DataMart at Mayo Clinic is a near real-time relational database with open-schema data feeds imported from electronic health records (EHR). Data domains included physiologic monitoring, laboratory and radiologic investigations, medication orders, and provider notes. The development phase consisted of a review of the literature to identify features of readmitted patients followed by the identification of a cohort of patients readmitted to the ICU.[3]

The SWIFT score predicts the likelihood that a patient will be readmitted within 24 hours of discharge from the ICU. The score is calculated from parameters readily available in the electronic medical record (EMR) and includes the ICU admission source; ICU length of stay; last PaO2/FiO2 measurement; last Glasgow coma scale score; and most recent PaCO2 value (Table 10.1). The range of possible SWIFT scores is 0 to 64. Scores with a value greater than 15 had a 50% sensitivity

Table 10.1   Average Number of Data Points Each Patient Accumulates over the Course of 24 Hours in the ICU

	Average Data Points Per Day	
	Per Patient	**Per 24-Bed ICU**
Labs	60	1,440
Drug orders	10	240
Microbiology	2	48
X-ray	2	48
Vitals	1950	46,800

and an 85% specificity for predicting ICU readmission within 24 hours.

A prospective before-after study was designed to evaluate the impact of the introduction of the SWIFT score into practice on readmission rates and on clinician discharge decision making at the time of morning rounds. It was hypothesized that the availability of the score would alter clinician decision making and reduce readmission rates in a medical ICU. The 7-day readmission rate in the study ICU was between 6% and 8% at that time and was a high priority target for reduction.

SWIFT Implementation

The clinical practice had identified the target for quality improvement, thus buy-in from clinical nursing and medical leadership was high. Education materials were targeted at the bedside providers, with nursing materials designed in close consultation with nursing quality improvement coaches and physician materials designed by the physician study investigators. This material was delivered in a series of small group and individual provider discussions. The SWIFT score was automatically calculated once per day at 6:45 am before morning rounds, printed out on a sheet of paper and distributed to the attending and nursing lead staff. The clinical staff were instructed to review the SWIFT score as part of the rounding process on patients they were considering for discharge that day. The bedside nurse recorded when the score was discussed and the impact it had on clinical decision making (enhanced communication with receiving team; transfer to a telemetry/monitored environment; discharge postponed).

Results

The impact of the SWIFT score on clinician discharge planning is illustrated as follows. The first observation to note is the low rate of utilization of the SWIFT score. Of the 1938 discharges observed during the 1 year post-implementation period, only 356 patients (18.4%) had a SWIFT score discussed during morning rounds. Interestingly, the impact of that discussion was to alter the decision-making process in some way in 30% of patients.

Given the low uptake of the score, the impact on patient outcomes was predictably less than expected. The 24-hour and 7-day readmission rates in the pre and post phase were not significantly different. Resource utilization was not significantly different between the groups. This held true for the whole group and a severity of illness (APACHE) matched subgroup.

Case Discussion

Having been closely involved in this study, the low rate of utilization and the impact on patient outcomes came somewhat as a surprise! But a careful review of the case study reveals a number of obvious and potentially avoidable failure points.

SWIFT Score

The performance of the SWIFT score was reasonable and was developed on a database of patients highly representative of the study population. As such, it was expected to be a reasonable predictor of risk of readmission to the ICU in this study. However, the intention of this study was to reduce readmission rates through the implementation of the tool at the point of care. For this to be effective, the SWIFT score must provide the clinician with actionable information that leads to an intervention which reduces the risk of readmission. When one looks at the patient features that contribute most to the SWIFT score prediction algorithm, we immediately see a problem—none of these features are easily modifiable and some of them are absolutely not modifiable! What action is a clinician to take when informed that the patient who spends a long time in the ICU and has come from a nursing home has a high risk of readmission to the ICU? Most will quickly discard the information and very soon after stop using the tool.

By calibrating the SWIFT score to a prediction of risk of readmission, we selected out information that was not actionable at the bedside. A more successful approach may have been to calibrate the SWIFT score to identify modifiable clinical features that, if acted upon, would reduce the risk of readmission. This is an important distinction and is one that we learned through this study to incorporate into our subsequent development efforts.

Study Design

The study was designed as a before-after study in a single center. This is a weak design for establishing both causality and generalizability. It is, however, an efficient and simple study design when resources are limited or you are gathering preliminary safety and efficacy data for a broader implementation effort. This approach tends to favor positive studies, however. If, for example, the SWIFT score was demonstrated in this environment to reduce readmission rates, there is no doubt that we would have proceeded to a broader implementation and study. In this case, the negative results meant that the tool never made it out of the medical ICU, which limits our ability to determine how large an impact the provider–patient–environment interactions contributed to the failure of the tool to impact on readmission rates. Would higher adoption rates have been observed in other ICUs? Would those higher adoption rates have translated into better outcomes for patients? We can only speculate.

A potentially better study design would have been a cluster randomization trial across several ICU settings. In this case, comparisons between ICUs could be made and more generalizable conclusions drawn.

Implementation

When designing tools to be used in clinical practice, resources must be committed to implementation up front. Part of the implementation effort requires that the developers clearly establish the stakeholders' requirements. In this case, we established the clinical leadership requirements but failed to understand the bedside provider's requirements. This led to a tool that successfully identified a high-risk readmission cohort but failed to make that information actionable at the bedside. A second key function of an implementation effort is to provide education on the use of the tool while establishing buy-in. In this case, our nursing quality improvement coaches took a lead and did a good job of engaging and educating nursing leadership and bedside nursing staff. The physician team leaders, that is, the authors, did not do an equally good job with the bedside physicians. The implementation effort for this group was less consistent. It is possible that a more concerted effort could have increased the adoption rate of the SWIFT score.

In addition to understanding the stakeholder's requirements and establishing their buy-in, the implementation team needs to successfully embed the tool into the workflow. In the case of the SWIFT score, very limited resources were dedicated to implementation. Hand delivering, once a day, a paper print-out of the calculated score to clinical staff was less than ideal. Providers can be difficult to track down, paper printouts get mislaid, and patients admitted after the list is printed are not included. The occasional server breakdown, dealt with during standard office hours, meant that there were occasions when the SWIFT score was not available on any patients. The delivery mechanism was therefore fragile and vulnerable to failure. This undermines clinician confidence, causes irritation, and makes it very difficult for clinical champions to lead the charge for adoption. A more robust delivery mechanism was not available at the time of the study, but integration into the electronic environment would potentially have overcome some of these implementation problems and increased the likelihood of SWIFT score adoption.

Results

The primary and secondary outcomes of this study were clearly defined up front. Both observational data and patient outcome data were gathered. The multimodal approach is very useful when one is trying to understand the contribution a tool such as the SWIFT score is making on a patient-centered outcome. In this case, we hypothesized that the availability of the SWIFT score would result in discussion at the bedside, which altered clinical decision making and reduced readmission rates. Even if patient readmission rates had plummeted, without data on adoption and impact on clinical decision making, it would not be possible to determine if the SWIFT score contributed in any way to the observed patient outcome. Direct field observation is a wonderful tool, but the cost of an observational study can be substantial. In the case of the

SWIFT study, this consumed most of the team resources. The consequence of this was less resources being available for the implementation effort. Some potential alternatives can be considered to reduce the strain on resources. In an electronic environment, log data can be used to estimate adoption. Structured interviews and validated survey instruments can be deployed to understand intention to use a technology, identify barriers to adoption, define stakeholder requirements, or understand the impact on clinical decision making and cognitive load. This can greatly reduce the observational burden and facilitate a more complete understanding of the success or failure of the instrument.

In the second case study, we examine how we applied some of the lessons learned from the SWIFT study and what impact that had on clinical practice and patient outcomes.

10.2 Case Study 2: Lessons Applied, More to Be Learned—AWARE Dashboard

The average patient in the ICU accumulates nearly 2000 data points per day as a result of his or her care (Table 10.1). Understanding that an attending physician may oversee the care of a large number of patients, one can appreciate that important information may be missed and that this may result in unintentional harm to the patient. This harm may be manifest as delayed or missed diagnosis, unreliable application of high-quality care, and errors of therapeutic intervention.

The EMR was introduced in part to capture and store large quantities of data in a legible fashion for use by the clinician. Despite their potential, commercially available EMRs remain stubbornly wedded to user interfaces that are poorly suited to the delivery of care at the bedside. Despite protests to the contrary by vendors, EMRs are not user friendly and can be tremendously frustrating for clinicians to use. Indeed, poor design of the EMR is increasingly recognized as an important contributor to patient harm and medical error.[4] This is particularly true in acute care environments where large amounts of data need to be processed and a rapidly evolving clinical picture demands that decisions be made quickly.

It was against this background that our group embarked on, what turned out to be, an 8-year journey to improve the point of care analysis and presentation of ICU data. The project came to be known as AWARE—Ambient Warning and Response Evaluation, and is the subject of the second case study.[5]

AWARE Design Principals

AWARE was designed using a human-centered design framework. During each stage of development and testing, the needs and limitations of end users were determined and the assumptions of the designers challenged. AWARE was designed primarily to address the information needs of clinicians engaged in the bedside care of critically ill patients. The information needs of clinicians were determined over an 18-month period through a combination of in situ observational study and expert opinion.[6] This study informed the data hierarchy for the user interface. Once the data hierarchy was established, the clinicians determined how best to organize the data for point of care use. The resulting single patient viewer, which was organized with all clinically relevant data, was presented by organ system on a single screen (Figure 10.1). Clicking on any data element provided access to underlying rich, time series data, images, or text. This had the advantage of allowing users to navigate from a common starting point through data in an infinite number of ways. This supports different clinical data–gathering styles and problem-solving approaches. Thus, from a single user

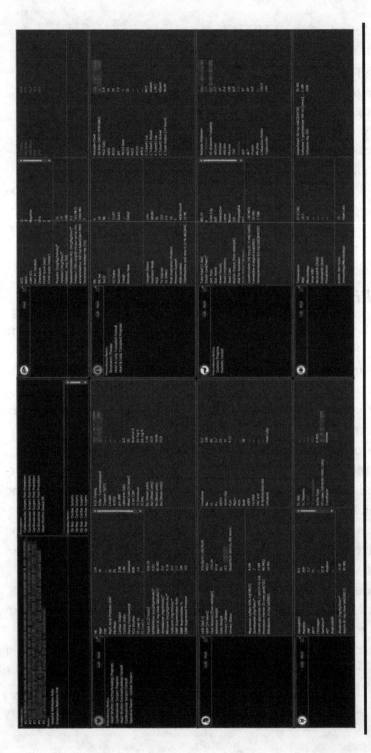

Figure 10.1 AWARE single patient screen.

interface, any number of clinical scenarios or providers could be accommodated without imposing a particular workflow on the end user.

At a later date, a multipatient viewer (Figure 10.2) was designed to facilitate situational awareness and high-level decision making. In this view, high priority data are further abstracted and presented as icons to end users to provide an overview of the severity of patients' illness, the emergence of new clinical problems, and the clinical workload of the entire ICU.

The face validity of the usefulness of AWARE was confirmed with end users at every stage of the design process. When a stable build of AWARE was ready, the AWARE team moved to the next phase in the human-centered design development process: testing.

Testing

The introduction of information technology (IT) into clinical practice brings with it risk. Critically ill patients are very vulnerable to delays in care or diagnosis. The clinical members of the design team were acutely aware of that risk and determined early on in the human-centered design process that testing of safety and efficacy was going to be a key determinant of success. The main steps in the testing and validation process included a technical review focused on the stability of data interfaces and validation of data integrity; an assessment of the impact on providers including cognitive load, efficiency, team safety, clinical performance, and usability assessment; the impact on processes of care; and finally the impact on patients.[7,8]

AWARE Implementation

The results from these evaluations were positive and AWARE was put into production in the clinical environment in July

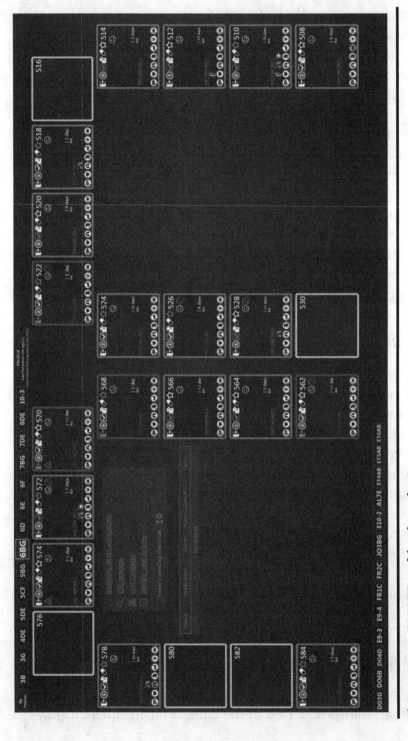

Figure 10.2 AWARE multipatient viewer.

2012. The uptick in clinical utilization over time is shown in Figure 10.3.

Adoption was greatly aided by the intuitive interface, measurable improvement in data presentation and data navigation, and the flexibility of the programming team to rapidly incorporate new functionality requested by frontline clinical users. Formal implementation efforts and rollout of additional functionality drove the steep rise in user numbers seen between November and December 2013.[9]

Results and Lessons Learned

In contrast to the SWIFT study outlined in Case 1, the introduction of AWARE into clinical practice was a resounding success. The interface was reliable, safe, and easy to use. Providers could access clinical data more efficiently with a measurable impact on clinician performance. Processes of care were more reliably completed. Patient outcomes have improved between the time the AWARE tool was initially rolled out and today, with ICU length of stay, hospital length of stay, and costs reduced significantly (publication is under revision).

The clinical problem that AWARE was solving was compelling for the providers and practice—how to deal with the deluge of information emanating from our increasingly complex patients and digital records? Clinical ICU leadership and bedside providers were the key initial stakeholders. Once a working prototype of AWARE was available, we got this into the hands of these key stakeholders. Demonstrations of AWARE working in real time, on live clinical data, firmly established buy-in from these stakeholders and facilitated a broader conversation within our healthcare organization. As we engaged in these conversations, the AWARE team gathered objective data using a combination of controlled laboratory experiments, small-scale pilot studies, and eventually step-wedge clinical trials. The results from these studies supported the hypothesis that AWARE could ameliorate the problem of data overload in the ICU environment.

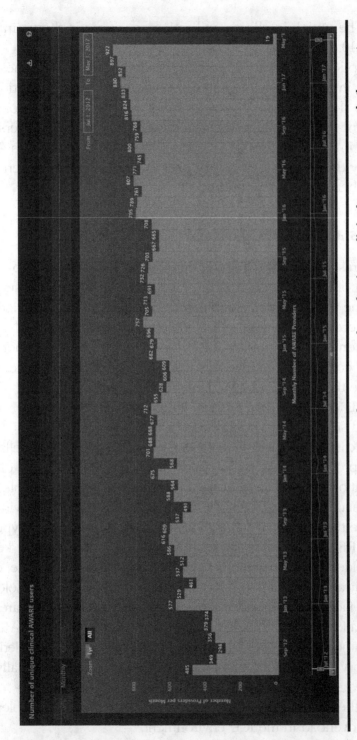

Figure 10.3 Number of software sessions per month (top). Number of unique clinical users per month (bottom).

Eight years later, AWARE is still going strong in practice, has been Food and Drug Administration (FDA) cleared as a 510k software medical device, and has been licensed to commercial vendors. The challenge for the future is to thrive in an environment increasingly dominated by a couple of high-cost EMR vendors.

10.3 Summary

Today, it is easier than ever to develop and promote healthcare ITs for clinical and administrative use. This combined with an increasingly competitive healthcare market is feeding an enormous growth in health IT offerings. It is very important that key decision makers within healthcare organizations understand the need to objectively evaluate the claims made for technologies before committing their organizations to one or other solution. The foregoing case scenarios are intended to bring to life the real-world challenges that decision makers are faced with when judging the validity of developers claims. This book is intended to provide a framework for the objective evaluation of those claims.

References

1. Gajic O, Malinchoc M, Comfere TB, et al. The stability and workload index for transfer score predicts unplanned intensive care unit patient readmission: Initial development and validation. *Crit Care Med*. 2008;36(3):676–682.
2. Herasevich V, Pickering BW, Dong Y, Peters SG, Gajic O. Informatics infrastructure for syndrome surveillance, decision support, reporting, and modeling of critical illness. *Mayo Clin Proc*. 2010;85(3):247–254.
3. Chandra S, Agarwal D, Hanson A, et al. The use of an electronic medical record based automatic calculation tool to quantify risk of unplanned readmission to the intensive care unit: A validation study. *J Crit Care*. 2011;6(6):634.e9–634.e15.

4. Carayon P, Wood KE. Patient safety: The role of human factors and systems engineering. *Stud Health Technol Inform*. 2010;153:23–46.

5. Pickering BW, Herasevich, VAB. Novel representation of clinical information in the ICU: Developing user interfaces which reduce information overload. *Appl Clin Inform*. 2010;1(2):116–131.

6. Pickering BW, Hurley K, Marsh B. Identification of patient information corruption in the intensive care unit: Using a scoring tool to direct quality improvements in handover. *Crit Care Med* 2009;37(11):2905–2912.

7. Ahmed A, Chandra S, Herasevich V, Gajic O, Pickering BW. The effect of two different electronic health record user interfaces on intensive care provider task load, errors of cognition, and performance. *Crit Care Med*. 2011;39(7):1626–1634.

8. Dziadzko MA, Herasevich V, Sen A, Pickering BW, Knight A-MA, Moreno Franco P. User perception and experience of the introduction of a novel critical care patient viewer in the ICU setting. *Int J Med Inform*. 2016;88:86–91.

9. Pickering BW, Dong Y, Ahmed A, et al. The implementation of clinician designed, human-centered electronic medical record viewer in the intensive care unit: A pilot step-wedge cluster randomized trial. *Int J Med Inform*. 2015;84(5):299–307.

Index

Absolute risk reduction (ARR), 76–77
Abstract, and evaluation project, 84, 96
Accuracy, of study design, 42–43
Active and passive evaluation, 113–116
Adverse events, 166
Agency for Healthcare Research and Quality (AHRQ), 10, 13–14, 106
AHRQ, *See* Agency for Healthcare Research and Quality (AHRQ)
American Recovery and Reinvestment Act (ARRA), 12
Analysis of variance (ANOVA), 71–72
Analytics methods, and evaluation data, 70–79
  ANOVA, 71–72
  assessing agreements, 74
  correlation, 70
  diagnostic accuracy studies, 72–74
  multiple comparisons, 77
  outcome measurements, 74–77
  regression, 70–71
  sample size calculation, 78
  statistical tools, 78–79

  subgroup analysis, 77–78
  time-to-event (survival analysis), 72
ANOVA, *See* Analysis of variance (ANOVA)
ARR, *See* Absolute risk reduction (ARR)
ARRA, *See* American Recovery and Reinvestment Act (ARRA)

Barcoding technologies, 112
Before-after study, 24, 158–159
Bias, study design, 44–45
Bland–Altman plot, 74

Care delivery organization (CDO), 118
Case-control studies, 26
Case series and reports, 26–27
Categorical variables, 61
CBA, *See* Cost-benefit analysis (CBA)
CCA, *See* Cost-consequence analysis (CCA)
CCHIT, *See* Certification Commission for Health Information Technology (CCHIT)
CDO, *See* Care delivery organization (CDO)

CEA, *See* Cost-effectiveness analysis (CEA)
Centers for Medicare and Medicaid Services (CMS), 106
Certification Commission for Health Information Technology (CCHIT), 11
CHEERS, *See* Consolidated Health Economic Evaluation Reporting Standards (CHEERS)
CI, *See* Confidence interval (CI)
CIF, *See* Common Industry Format (CIF)
Clinical epidemiology evidence pyramid, 24–27
Clinical outcome measures, 48
Clinical process measurements, 48–49
Clinical research design
    clinical epidemiology evidence pyramid, 24–27
    considerations in HIT, 27–29
    diagnostic performance study, 31
    overview, 23–24
    RCT and, 29–31
"A Clinician's Guide to Cost-Effectiveness Analysis," 135
CMA, *See* Cost-minimization analysis (CMA)
CMS, *See* Centers for Medicare and Medicaid Services (CMS)
Cogan, Thomas, 3
Cognitive walk-through, 175–176
    procedure, 176–178
Cohort studies, 26
Common Industry Format (CIF), 121
Comparisons groups, 68–69
Composite outcome, 51
Computerized physician order entry (CPOE), 7, 105, 112
Computer-stored ambulatory record (COSTAR), 7

Computer vision syndrome (CVS), 75
Confidence interval (CI), 64–65, 159
Confounding, study design, 45
Consolidated Health Economic Evaluation Reporting Standards (CHEERS), 91, 138–143
Consolidated Standards of Reporting Trials (CONSORT), 91
CONSORT, *See* Consolidated Standards of Reporting Trials (CONSORT)
Continuous variables, 61
Correlation analysis, 70
COSTAR, *See* Computer-stored ambulatory record (COSTAR)
Cost-benefit analysis (CBA), 127, 129, 133–134
Cost-consequence analysis (CCA), 127, 129
Cost-effectiveness analysis (CEA), 129, 134–136
"Cost-Effectiveness of Telemonitoring for High-Risk Pregnant Women," 136
Cost evaluation
    cost-benefit analysis (CBA), 133–134
    cost-effectiveness analysis (CEA), 134–136
    cost-minimization analysis (CMA), 136–137
    health economics basics
        measure and outcomes, 131–133
        overview, 127–129
        setting and methodology, 129–131
    overview, 125–127
    reporting, 138–144

return on investment (ROI), 137–138
Cost-minimization analysis (CMA), 129, 136–137
Cost-utility analysis (CUA), 129
CPOE, *See* Computerized physician order entry (CPOE)
Cross-sectional (descriptive) studies, 26
CUA, *See* Cost-utility analysis (CUA)
CVS, *See* Computer vision syndrome (CVS)

Data collection, for study design, 53–54
Data distribution, 61–64
Data preparation, 61
Data quality, and study design, 54–56
Descriptive (summary) statistics, 61
Diagnostic accuracy studies, 72–74
Diagnostic performance, 25–26
Diagnostic performance study, 31
Diagrams, and evaluation project, 97–99
Dichotomous variables, 61
Dissemination methods, of evaluation project, 84–86

EBM, *See* Evidence-based medicine (EBM)
Eclipsys, 7
EDI, *See* Electronic data interchange (EDI)
Effectiveness evaluation
efficacy and (*see* Efficacy and effectiveness evaluation)
usability and, 165–166
Efficacy and effectiveness evaluation
before-after study, 158–159
gold standard validation study, 157–158

methodology, 153–155
outcome evaluation, 150–152
overview, 147–149
security evaluation, 159–161
settings for, 152–153
survey analysis study, 155–157
timing, 155
EHR, *See* Electronic health record (EHR)
Electromagnetic radiation emitting devices (ERED), 12
Electronic data interchange (EDI), 159
Electronic health record (EHR), 4, 20, 105, 166
usability evaluation and, 170–173
HIT and, 171–173
Electronic medical record (EMR), 1, 105, 168–170
EMR, *See* Electronic medical record (EMR)
Enhancing the QUAlity and Transparency Of health Research (EQUATOR), 91
EQUATOR, *See* Enhancing the QUAlity and Transparency Of health Research (EQUATOR)
ERED, *See* Electromagnetic radiation emitting devices (ERED)
Error evaluation, and usability, 165–166
Error root causes, 166
Evaluation, HIT
Agency for Healthcare Research and Quality (AHRQ), 13–14
definitions, 7–8
Food and Drug Administration (FDA), 12
fundamental steps for, 14–16
health information technology assessment, 10

health technology assessment
(HTA), 9
medical technology assessment
(MTA), 9
purpose of, 2–4
regulatory framework, 11–14
structure and design, 20
technology assessment, 9
usability, 171–173
Evaluation data analysis
overview, 59–60
statistical tests
analytics methods, 70–79
hypothesis testing, 66–67
non-parametric tests, 67
number of comparisons
groups, 68–69
one- and two-tailed tests,
67–68
overview, 66
paired and independent
tests, 68
statistics principles
confidence interval (CI),
64–65
data distribution, 61–64
data preparation, 61
descriptive (summary)
statistics, 61
overview, 60–61
p-value, 65
Evaluation project report
abstract and, 96
and diagrams and, 97–99
dissemination methods, 84–86
evaluation report and, 96
information visualization/
infographics and, 99–100
oral presentations and, 101–102
overview, 83–84
poster and, 96–97
scalable format and, 102
scientific papers and, 86–91

software and, 100–101
standards and guidelines,
91–96
target audience, 84
Evaluation questions, 31–35
Evaluation report, 84, 96
Evaluative indicators, 166
Evidence-based medicine (EBM),
24, 74
Explanatory trials, 148

FDA, *See* Food and Drug
Administration (FDA)
FDASIA, *See* Food and Drug
Administration Safety and
Innovation Act (FDASIA)
Financial impact measures, 49–51
Food and Drug Administration
(FDA), 12, 29, 74, 106
Food and Drug Administration
Safety and Innovation Act
(FDASIA), 108
Food, Drug, and Cosmetic Act, 12

Gold standard validation study,
157–158
Government organizations, and
safety evaluation
legislative process and, 109–110
meaningful use (Stage 2), 109
ONC EHR Technology
Certification Program, 109
overview, 106–108
standards and certification
criteria (2014 Edition), 109
GraphPad Prism tool, 79

Hawes, William, 3
Health and Human Services (HHS),
107, 161
Healthcare Information and
Management Systems
Society (HIMSS), 169

Healthcare information technology
(HIT)
    clinical research design
        considerations in, 27–29
    evaluation
        Agency for Healthcare
            Research and Quality
            (AHRQ), 13–14
        definitions, 7–8
        Food and Drug
            Administration (FDA), 12
        fundamental steps for, 14–16
        health information technology
            assessment, 10
        health technology assessment
            (HTA), 9
        medical technology
            assessment (MTA), 9
        purpose of, 2–4
        regulatory framework, 11–14
        structure and design, 20
        technology assessment, 9
        usability, 171–173
Health economics basics
    measure and outcomes, 131–133
    overview, 127–129
    setting and methodology,
        129–131
Health information exchange
    (HIE), 5
Health information technology
    assessment, 10
Health Information Technology
    for Economic and Clinical
    Health (HITECH) Act,
    11–12
Health Insurance Portability and
    Accountability Act of 1996
    (HIPPA), 159
"Health IT Hazard Manager Beta-
    Test: Final Report," 116
Health-related quality of life
    (HRQOL), 52

Health technology assessment
    (HTA), 9
Heuristic evaluation, 179–181
HHS, *See* Health and Human
    Services (HHS)
HIE, *See* Health information
    exchange (HIE)
HIMSS, *See* Healthcare Information
    and Management Systems
    Society (HIMSS)
HIPPA, *See* Health Insurance
    Portability and
    Accountability Act of 1996
    (HIPPA)
HITECH, *See* Health Information
    Technology for Economic
    and Clinical Health
    (HITECH) Act
HRQOL, *See* Health-related quality
    of life (HRQOL)
HTA, *See* Health technology
    assessment (HTA)
Human–computer interaction, 110
Hypothesis testing, 66–67

ICU, *See* Intensive care unit (ICU)
Independent tests, 68
Information visualization/
    infographics, 99–100
Institute of Medicine (IOM), 107
Institutional Review Board (IRB), 88
The Institution for Affording
    Immediate Relief to
    Persons Apparently Dead
    From Drowning, 3
Intensive care unit (ICU), 68, 121
Intermediate outcome, 51
Interquartile range (IQR), 63–64, 89
IOM, *See* Institute of Medicine
    (IOM)
IQR, *See* Interquartile range (IQR)
IRB, *See* Institutional Review Board
    (IRB)

JMP tool, 79
Journal of Medical Economics, 5

Kappa, 74
Keystroke-level model (KLM),
178–179
KLM, *See* Keystroke-level model
(KLM)

Legislative process, and safety
evaluation, 109–110
Length-of-stay (LOS), 136
Linear regression, 70
Logistics regression, 71
LOS, *See* Length-of-stay (LOS)

Meaningful use (Stage 2), 109
Measurement variables, 45–47
MedCalc tool, 79
Medical technology assessment
(MTA), 9
Microsoft Health Common User
Interface (MSCUI), 173
MSCUI, *See* Microsoft Health
Common User Interface
(MSCUI)
MTA, *See* Medical technology
assessment (MTA)
Multiple comparisons, 77
Multiple regression, 71
MUMPS programming language, 7

NAHIT, *See* National Alliance
for Health Information
Technology (NAHIT)
NASA-task load index
(NASA-TLX), 122
NASA-TLX, *See* NASA-task load
index (NASA-TLX)
National Alliance for Health
Information Technology
(NAHIT), 4
Negative predictive values (NPV), 158

Newsletter article, 86
Nominal variables, 61
Non-parametric tests, 67
NPV, *See* Negative predictive values
(NPV)

Objective measurements, 52–53
OCR, *See* Office for Civil Rights
(OCR)
Office for Civil Rights (OCR), 161
Office of Technology Assessment
(OTA), 9
Office of the General Counsel
(OGC), 161
Office of the National Coordinator
(ONC), 161
OGC, *See* Office of the General
Counsel (OGC)
ONC, *See* Office of the National
Coordinator (ONC)
ONC EHR Technology Certification
Program, 12, 109
One- and two-tailed tests, 67–68
Oral presentations, and evaluation
project, 101–102
Ordinal variables, 61
OTA, *See* Office of Technology
Assessment (OTA)
Outcome evaluation, 150–152
Outcome measurements, 74–77
Outliers, 63

Paired tests, 68
Passive and active evaluation,
113–116
Patient engagement tools, 111
Patient-reported outcome (PRO),
51–52
Percentiles, 63
Personal health records
(PHRs), 107
PHI, *See* Protected health
information (PHI)

PHRs, *See* Personal health records (PHRs)
Positive predictive values (PPV), 158
Poster, and evaluation project, 96–97
PPV, *See* Positive predictive values (PPV)
Pragmatic trials, 148
Precision, of study design, 42–43
Predictive values, 73
PRO, *See* Patient-reported outcome (PRO)
Probability theory, 63
Problem identification, and safety evaluation, 111–116
Prognosis, 77
Protected health information (PHI), 160
p-value, 65

QALYs, *See* Quality-adjusted life years (QALYs)
Qualitative data, 23, 61
Quality-adjusted life years (QALYs), 126
Quantitative data, 23, 61

Randomized controlled trial (RCT), 15, 23–25, 75, 91
  clinical research design and, 29–31 [bring back to previous line?]
Range and percentiles, 63
RCT, *See* Randomized controlled trial (RCT)
Receiver operating characteristic (ROC) curve, 73
Regression analysis, 70–71
Relative risk (RR), 159
Relative risk reduction (RRR), 76
Reporting
  cost evaluation, 138–144
  evaluation project

abstract and, 96
diagrams and, 97–99
dissemination methods, 84–86
evaluation report and, 96
information visualization/infographics and, 99–100
oral presentations and, 101–102
overview, 83–84
poster and, 96–97
scalable format and, 102
scientific papers and, 86–91
software and, 100–101
standards and guidelines, 91–96
target audience, 84
usability evaluation, 181
Return on investment (ROI), 129, 137–138
Risk parameters, 166
ROC, *See* Receiver operating characteristic (ROC) curve
ROI, *See* Return on investment (ROI)
RR, *See* Relative risk (RR)
RRR, *See* Relative risk reduction (RRR)
"The SAFER Guides: Empowering organizations to improve the safety and effectiveness of electronic health records," 116

Safety evaluation
  overview, 105–106
  passive and active evaluation, 113–116
  problem identification and, 111–116
  role of government organizations
    legislative process and, 109–110
    meaningful use (Stage 2), 109

ONC EHR Technology
Certification Program, 109
overview, 106–108
standards and certification
criteria (2014 Edition), 109
simulation studies and testing,
120–122
tools and methodologies,
116–122
Sample size calculation, 78
SAS tool, 78–79
Scalable format, and evaluation
project, 102
Scientific papers, and evaluation
project, 86–91
Scientific peer-reviewed article, 84
SD, *See* Standard deviation (SD)
Security evaluation, 159–161
Security risk assessment tool (SRA
tool), 161
Selection criteria, for study design,
39–41
Software, and evaluation project,
100–101
Software product Quality
Requirements and
Evaluation (SQuaRE), 121
SPSS tool, 79
SQuaRE, *See* Software product
Quality Requirements and
Evaluation (SQuaRE)
SRA tool, *See* Security risk
assessment tool (SRA tool)
Stakeholders, and evaluation
studies, 20–21
Standard deviation (SD), 63
Standards and certification criteria
(2014 Edition), 109
Standards and guidelines, 86, 91–96
"Statistical Guidance on Reporting
Results from Studies
Evaluating Diagnostic
Tests," 74

Statistical tests, and evaluation data
analytics methods, 70–79
ANOVA, 71–72
assessing agreements, 74
correlation, 70
diagnostic accuracy studies,
72–74
multiple comparisons, 77
outcome measurements,
74–77
regression, 70–71
sample size calculation, 78
statistical tools, 78–79
subgroup analysis, 77–78
time-to-event (survival
analysis), 72
hypothesis testing, 66–67
non-parametric tests, 67
number of comparisons groups,
68–69
one- and two-tailed tests, 67–68
overview, 66
paired and independent tests, 68
Statistical tools, 78–79
*Statistics for People Who (Think
They) Hate Statistics,* 59
Statistics principles, and evaluation
data
confidence interval (CI), 64–65
data distribution, 61–64
data preparation, 61
descriptive (summary)
statistics, 61
overview, 60–61
p-value, 65
Strengthening the Reporting of
Observational Studies
in Epidemiology
(STROBE), 96
STROBE, *See* Strengthening the
Reporting of Observational
Studies in Epidemiology
(STROBE)

Structure and design, of evaluation studies
  clinical research design
    clinical epidemiology
      evidence pyramid, 24–27
    considerations in HIT, 27–29
    diagnostic performance study, 31
    overview, 23–24
    RCT and, 29–31
  evaluation questions and, 31–35
  HIT and, 20
  overview, 19–20
  prioritizing study questions and, 21–23
  stakeholders and, 20–21
Study design and measurements
  accuracy and precision, 42–43
  bias, 44–45
  clinical outcome measures, 48
  clinical process measurements, 48–49
  composite outcome, 51
  confounding, 45
  data collection for, 53–54
  data quality, 54–56
  financial impact measures, 49–51
  health-related quality of life (HRQOL), 52
  intermediate outcome, 51
  measurement variables, 45–47
  overview, 37–39
  patient-reported outcome (PRO), 51–52
  selection criteria and sample, 39–41
  subjective and objective measurements, 52–53
  validity, 41–42
Subgroup analysis, 77–78
Subjective measurements, 52–53
Summary (descriptive) statistics, 61
Survey analysis study, 155–157

Survival/time-to-event analysis, 72
Systematic reviews, 24
System usability scale (SUS), 181–183

Tableau tool, 79
Target audience, and evaluation project, 84
Task, user, representation, and function (TURF), 175
Technology assessment, 9
Testing, usability evaluation, 173–175
  cognitive walk-through, 175–178
  heuristic evaluation, 179–181
  keystroke-level model (KLM), 178–179
  reporting, 181
  system usability scale (SUS), 181–183
Time-to-event/survival analysis, 72
Timing, and efficacy evaluation, 155
Tobacco smoke enema, 3
TURF, *See* Task, user, representation, and function (TURF)

UCD, *See* User-centered design (UCD)
Usability evaluation
  effectiveness and error evaluation, 165–166
  efficiency, 164
  EHR and, 170–173
    HIT and, 171–173
  electronic medical record (EMR), 168–170
  overview, 163–164
  testing approaches, 173–175
    cognitive walk-through, 175–178
    heuristic evaluation, 179–181
    keystroke-level model (KLM), 178–179

reporting, 181
system usability scale (SUS),
181–183
user satisfaction, 166–168
User-centered design (UCD), 109
User satisfaction, 166–168

Validity, of study design, 41–42
VDTs, *See* Visual Display Terminals
(VDTs)

Visual Display Terminals (VDTs), 175
Voluntary certification program, 109

Washington Patient Safety Coalition
(WPSC), 105
Website publication, 86
Weed, Larry, 7
World Bank, 135
WPSC, *See* Washington Patient
Safety Coalition (WPSC)

Printed in the United States
by Baker & Taylor Publisher Services